What STYLE is it?

What STYLE is it?

A • GUIDE • TO • AMERICAN • ARCHITECTURE

Building Watchers Series

JOHN C. POPPELIERS S. ALLEN CHAMBERS, JR. NANCY B. SCHWARTZ

HISTORIC AMERICAN BUILDINGS SURVEY
NATIONAL PARK SERVICE
U.S. DEPARTMENT OF THE INTERIOR
OUACHITA TECHNICAL COLLEGE

THE PRESERVATION PRESS

The Preservation Press
National Trust for Historic Preservation
1785 Massachusetts Avenue, N.W.
Washington, D.C. 20036

The National Trust for Historic Preservation is the only private, nonprofit national organization chartered by Congress to encourage public participation in the preservation of sites, buildings and objects significant in American history and culture. Support is provided by membership dues, endowment funds, contributions and grants from federal agencies, including the U.S. Department of the Interior, under provisions of the National Historic Preservation Act of 1966.

Printed in the United States of America
87 86   5

Library of Congress Cataloging in Publication Data

Poppeliers, John C.
  What style is it?

  Bibliography: p.
  1. Architecture—United States—Themes, motives.
I. Chambers, S. Allen.   II. Schwartz, Nancy B.
III. Historic American Buildings Survey.   IV. Title.
NA705.P6 1983   720'.973   83-19278
ISBN 0-89133-116-6

Unless otherwise noted, all photographs and measured drawings are part of the HABS collection.
Illustrations for the glossary were done by Matthew J. Mosca.

Designed by Anne Masters
Composed in Trump Medieval by Mid-Atlantic Photo Composition, Baltimore, Md., and printed on 70# Frostbrite by Collins Lithographing Inc., Baltimore, Md.

NA
705
.P6
1983

Contents

Acknowledgments

On the premise that to know architecture is to appreciate it—and to want to save it—the National Trust for Historic Preservation in 1976 asked the Historic American Buildings Survey to prepare a pictorial, nontechnical introduction to American architecture as a Bicentennial feature for its members. This four-part feature, which later became this book, *What Style Is It?*, appeared in the National Trust magazine, *Historic Preservation*, in 1976 and 1977. HABS was approached because of its preeminent role as the leading documentor of American architecture since 1933. *What Style Is It?* became not only one of the most popular features in *Historic Preservation*, it also has remained one of the most popular books published by the Preservation Press, going through six printings before this new, revised edition was published.

The text and illustrations for *What Style Is It?* were prepared by John Poppeliers, then chief of HABS and now director of the Division of Cultural Heritage, Culture Sector, Unesco; S. Allen Chambers, Jr., then and now an architectural historian with HABS and author of *Lynchburg: An Architectural History* (University Press of Virginia, 1981); and Nancy B. Schwartz, formerly a HABS architectural historian. John A. Burns and Lucy Pope Wheeler of HABS assisted in preparation of the chapters on Art Deco and the International Style. Matthew J. Mosca, a restoration architect formerly on the National Trust staff, assisted with preparation of the glossary.

For the revised edition, the Preservation Press gratefully acknowledges the assistance of Robert J. Kapsch, chief of HABS/HAER, and S. Allen Chambers, Jr., who provided text additions as well as new photographs and drawings. Staff of the Library of Congress Prints and Photographs Division who facilitated the ordering of new and replacement illustrations included Mary Ison, Joyce Nalewajk and Carol Johnson. This revised edition was published under the direction of Diane Maddex, editor, Preservation Press books, assisted by Gretchen Smith, associate editor. ■

Preface

The Historic American Buildings Survey, which marked its 50th anniversary in 1983, has documented more than 16,000 significant examples of America's historic architecture. Established in 1933 in part as a Depression-era program to employ out-of-work architects, HABS filled a need in this country to create a comprehensive record of American architectural achievements. HABS, in cooperation with the American Institute of Architects, the Library of Congress and others, has produced a national architectural archive in the form of photographs, measured drawings and written, historical information. An allied recording program, the Historic American Engineering Record, was initiated in 1969 to document the nation's exemplary engineering accomplishments.

As a tribute to the half century of work carried out by HABS, in 1983 the National Trust for Historic Preservation presented its highest honor, the Louise du Pont Crowninshield Award, to HABS. This award is only one manifestation of the many collaborative efforts of HABS and the National Trust to further the preservation and documentation of historic buildings in the United States.

What Style Is It? is another. In conjunction with the 50th anniversary, HABS and the National Trust have joined again to produce a revised edition of this popular guide to the styles that have created a rich architectural heritage for the United States. The text remains generally as originally written, with the addition of the chapter on bungalows and expansion of the chapter on period houses.

Since this book was originally published, however, HABS has continued to record significant structures, and some of its recent photographs are even better examples of the styles discussed than those used in the original edition. Consequently, a number of photographs have been replaced. And, although photographic coverage has always played a vital role in the HABS documentation program, an even more integral component is the measured drawing. Drawings are included here for the first time, to illustrate clearly the features of the styles as only such drawings can, as well as to show the scope of the HABS documents that record American architecture.

One of the important features of the HABS collection is that it is accessible to the public. Housed at the Library of Congress, the collection is available for review during library hours. In addition, all the material may be reproduced through the library's Photoduplication Service. More detailed information on how to use the collection is given on page 111.

Obviously, style is an essential element of the study and classification of architecture, but it should by no means be considered the only basis on which to judge a building. As HABS moves into its second half century of recording buildings that reflect the richness of American creativity, attention will be focused on other equally important aspects, such as structural considerations, technological advances and other factors that have received less attention than they deserve. And, as it has in the past, HABS will continue to record vernacular architecture as well as "high-style" examples.

HABS looks forward to its next 50 years of recording America's architectural heritage. The achievements attained so far have been truly impressive; we hope that HABS's influence—in documentation as well as in preservation—will be as notable as it approaches its centennial. ∎

S. Allen Chambers, Jr.
Historic American Buildings Survey
January 1984

Introduction

"Style"** is one of the most used—and abused—words in the English language, particularly when pressed into service in the study of architectural history. Defining the word "style" itself is the first hurdle encountered in the preparation of a guide to American architectural styles. This book attempts to bring some order to semantic confusion and to illustrate examples of styles that have flourished in the continental United States since the first colonial settlements. The following definition of architectural style from the *Oxford English Dictionary* has been used: "a definite type of architecture, distinguished by special characteristics of structure and ornament." Conceived in these terms, style is essentially visual and has no necessary relationship to the function of a building—churches, courthouses and residences may all be of the same architectural style.

Stylistic designations aid in describing architecture and in relating buildings—even of different chronological periods—to one another. But more than that, stylistic classification acknowledges that building is not just a craft; it is an art form that reflects the philosophy, intellectual currents, hopes and aspirations of its time.

Like most other manifestations of social change, stylistic periods do not have sharp edges. It is tempting to subdivide them into early, middle, late, neo- and protostyles. However, for anyone interested in identifying, enjoying and defending the architectural assets of a building or community, the real need is to understand the broad stylistic movements in American architecture.

To be useful, stylistic nomenclature should describe visual features. However, many long-established terms, such as "colonial" and "Victorian," refer essentially to historical and political periods and tell little about a building's appearance. Thus, the word "colonial," for instance, can be applied with equal validity to the

House of the Seven Gables (c. 1668) in Salem, Mass., with its rambling medieval appearance, and Mount Pleasant (1762) in Philadelphia, which illustrates the restrained adaptation of classical Renaissance forms. "Colonial" is also used in modern real estate jargon to describe late 19th- and 20th-century structures that include such familiar 18th-century motifs as exterior shutters, Palladian windows and broken pediment doorways. Obviously, a term that can be so freely applied is not useful as a stylistic designation.

Other widely used architectural labels such as "Georgian" and "Federal," which are also derived from historical periods, elicit fairly specific visual images. The Wren Building (begun in 1695) in Williamsburg, Va., and Hampton Plantation (1783–90) in Towson, Md., fit the description of Georgian even though they were not built between 1714 and 1775, when the Georges of England ruled the American colonies.

Many buildings also defy stylistic labels. They may represent transitional periods when one style was slowly blending into another; they may exhibit the conscious combination of unrelated stylistic elements for a certain effect; or they may be the product of pure whimsy or eccentricity. Such buildings are especially common in the United States, where many early structures were produced by competent but unsophisticated builders far removed from the European origins of current styles.

Many of the buildings pictured here represent the most costly and sophisticated of their period, for the designers of such buildings would most consciously have adhered to the dictates of fashion. These structures also served as models for simpler buildings.

Some styles enjoyed periods of revival. The people of the 19th century had a special romantic predilection for resurrecting historic styles more or—usually—less faithful to the originals and giving them a new life. They turned to the ancient styles of Greece, Rome and Europe and to the American colonial period. To fully appreciate the influence of a style, its revivals as well as its prototypes must be considered. ■

EARLY COLONIAL

Few structures remain from the first English settlements on the East Coast, and those that do exhibit marked regional variations. The term "late medieval" is perhaps the most adequate general designation because it acknowledges the traditional qualities of 17th-century English colonial architecture. St. Luke's Church (1632), Smithfield, Va., for example, resembles an English Gothic parish church. Other early English colonial buildings in North America reflect styles that were developed during the reigns of Elizabeth I (1558–1603) and James I (1603–25) combining medieval verticality and steep, picturesque rooflines with classical ornament and symmetry of plan and fenestration. In the ample but plain house of the English yeoman—a late 16th-century building type that was the model for most colonial residences—the predominance of medieval forms is evident; this type is characterized by a steeply pitched roof, tall, massive chimneys and small windows with leaded casements.

In New England, where hardwoods were plentiful, the massive hewn and pegged house frame was almost universal. Spaces between boards were filled with brick nogging or wattle and daub (twigs and clay). In England this construction often was left exposed, creating the effect known as half-timbering. In New England, however, this structural wall system was always sheathed in clapboards. Second-story overhangs, central chimneys and the sloping lean-tos of the familiar saltbox (usually added later) were also common features.

In the southern colonies, one-story houses (often brick) with end chimneys were predominant in the 17th century. An exception is the two-story Bacon's Castle (1655) in

St. Luke's Church (1632), near Smithfield, Va., has hallmarks of the English Gothic parish church—prominent tower, steep roof, buttresses and lancet-arched windows. New Englanders rejected the Anglican model and developed the plain, square meetinghouse to symbolize their dissenting views. (John O. Bostrup)

Bacon's Castle (1655), Surrey County,
Va., is the best American example of
early 17th-century English architecture.
The dramatically grouped chimney
stacks are direct transplants from the
settlers' homeland, while the cur-
vilinear Flemish gables show Continental influences. (Jack E. Boucher)

The House of the Seven Gables (c. 1668), Salem, Mass., reflects a tradition of
building in wood that was brought to New England by Puritan colonists from
eastern English counties. It is more asymmetrical than other clapboard English
houses, but it shares with them the steep roofline, decorative overhang, massive central chimneys, casement windows and two-story height. (Richard Cheek)

The Elihu Coleman House (1722), Nantucket Island, Mass., is typical of early New England houses, with its prominent central chimney, shingle covering and lean-to, or saltbox, configuration. (Cortlandt V. D. Hubbard)

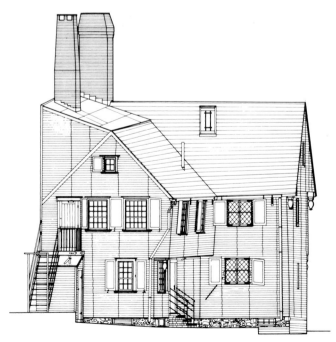

The Paul Revere House (1678–80), Boston, sole survivor of the city's 17th-century row houses, was originally one unit in a two-story gable-roofed row. Its picturesque appearance owes much to an early 20th-century restoration. (Laura L. Hochuli)

Surry County, Va., the major remaining 17th-century house with a modicum of sophistication. Its decorative gables and picturesque chimneys made it as stylish as the small manor houses of English gentry.

While the late medieval style dominated American architecture during the 17th century, major stylistic changes were sweeping England. Although Inigo Jones (1573–1652) had designed earlier English buildings in the Italian Renaissance manner, the return of the Stuart monarchy from exile on the Continent and the necessity of rebuilding London after the fire of 1666 brought Renaissance styles fully to bear on English architecture. The stylistic revolution came to the American colonies at the turn of the 18th century with the popularity of Georgian architecture. ■

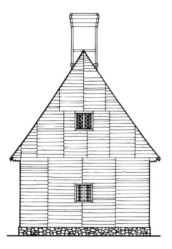

The Day-Breedon House (c. 1700), near Lusby in Calvert County, Md., shows the steep roof and small windows with leaded casements typical of early colonial architecture on the eastern seaboard. (Cary Carson and Chinh Hoang)

The Adam Thoroughgood House (1636–40), Virginia Beach, Va., has massive T-shaped chimneys, a steep gable, two-room plan and leaded casements characterizing the end of the medieval building tradition. End chimneys and brick construction were common in the southern colonies. (H. J. Sheely)

Magnolia Mound (c. 1790), Baton Rouge, La., reflects the architectural traditions established several decades earlier by French colonists. A raised cottage, the house has a prominent gallery shaded by an extension of the hipped roof, an adaptation to the humid climate of the lower Mississippi valley. (Willie Graham and Kate Johns)

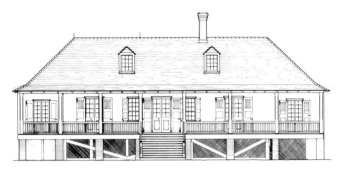

The Kautz Barn (c. 1877), near Shaw-
nee, Pa., is a product of the area's long
tradition of Germanic folk architecture.
(William H. Edwards)

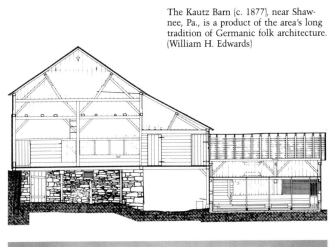

The African House (c. 1820), Melrose, La., is part of Melrose Plantation, which
was established and developed over many generations by free blacks. One of
several buildings in the complex thought to have African design origins, this
structure's overpowering hipped roof conceals a second story. (Lester Jones)

The Dutch Reformed Church (c. 1700),
North Tarrytown, N.Y., has a bell-
shaped gambrel roof that marks it as
unmistakably Dutch colonial. Washington Irving, who is buried in the
churchyard, made the site famous in
"The Legend of Sleepy Hollow."
(Jack E. Boucher)

GEORGIAN

Although certain old standard architectural history books extend the Georgian period in American architecture until 1830 (the end of the reign of George IV), most scholars now agree that the style generally terminated in America with the Revolutionary War. It began about 1700 with construction of the Wren Building (begun in 1695) at the College of William and Mary and, soon after, the Governor's Palace and the Capitol in Williamsburg, Va., both of which have been reconstructed. All three exhibited hallmarks of Georgian design: rigid symmetry, axial entrances, geometrical proportions, hipped roofs and sash windows.

The Georgian style reflected Renaissance ideals made popular in England by architect Sir Christopher Wren. Renaissance influences arrived there first by way of the Netherlands and then in 1715 through Leoni's first English publication of the works of Italian architect Andrea Palladio. The work of Wren and his followers was based on that of Italian architects of the 16th century, especially Palladio, who in turn had freely adapted Roman classical forms.

These stylistic changes gradually spread to the other side of the Atlantic. Leoni's 1715 edition of Palladio's *Works* was followed by a host of other handbooks, all destined to influence American building arts and to increase the academic, formal quality of the Georgian style. Colen Campbell's *Vitruvius Britannicus* (1715–25), James Gibbs's *Book of Architecture* (1728), William Salmon's *Palladio Londinensis* (1734) and Robert Morris's *Select Architecture* (1757) were among them. If Westover (begun in 1730) in Charles City County, Va., incorporated only a door or a mantel from Salmon's publication, Mount Airy, Warsaw, Va., built some 30 years later in 1758–62, owes its entire facade to a plate in Gibbs.

Features of Palladian design that were prevalent in the mid-Georgian period include giant pilasters marking the corners of buildings and the double or two-story portico, first seen in America at Drayton Hall (1738–42), a National Trust property near Charleston, S.C. In simpler buildings, this central emphasis took the form of a central pavilion with pediment and pilasters as at the Vassall-Craigie-Longfellow House (1759), Cambridge, Mass. It was also from Palladio that builders of colonial country estates, especially those in Maryland and Virginia, borrowed the idea of the five-part composition, consisting of a central block with connected dependencies. The Palladian window—a large arched central

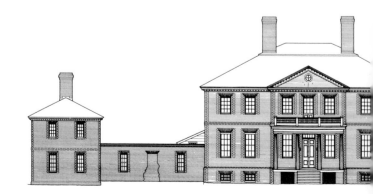

The Wren Building (1695), College of William and Mary, Williamsburg, Va., is one of the earliest American Georgian buildings. Named for the English architect, its axiality, geometrical proportions, central pavilion and belt course are Georgian features. (Colonial Williamsburg Foundation)

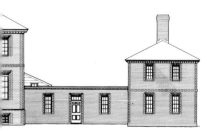

Blandfield (1769–73), Essex County, Va., is one of Virginia's most impressive Georgian manors, clearly demonstrating the Palladian five-part composition of a central block connected by hyphens to identical dependencies. (Rebecca Trumbull)

window flanked by narrower rectangular windows—was also borrowed wholesale by American builders.

The hiatus of construction during the Revolutionary War essentially ended the Georgian period of architecture in America, although conservative builders continued to use the style into the 19th century. Many handsome, commodious Georgian buildings along the eastern seaboard served as homes of the founders of the nation and were sites of historic events of the Revolutionary War.

It is not surprising, then, that after 75 years of reviving European styles, late 19th-century American architects inspired by post-Centennial zeal began to look to their own national past for appropriate models. In their eagerness to ensure that the design heritage would be recognized, the

The Vassall-Craigie-Longfellow House (1759), Cambridge, Mass., has a projecting central pavilion, emphasized by Ionic pilasters, which was still a much-used feature of Georgian design more than 50 years after the Wren Building was constructed. (Jack E. Boucher)

Mount Pleasant (1761), Philadelphia, has a Palladian window in the center of its facade. This High Renaissance motif occurred in Philadelphia as early as 1727 in Christ Church, but its general use in American Georgian design did not come until several decades later. (Cortlandt V. D. Hubbard)

Drayton Hall (1738–42), near Charleston, S.C., has probably the first American example of a Palladian double portico. The raised basement is particularly appropriate to the climate and topography of the South Carolina Low Country. (Frances Benjamin Johnston, Library of Congress)

architects often exaggerated their case. They also had to find ways to apply 18th-century details to buildings that were decidedly 19th-century in size and function, such as railroad stations and public schools. To accomplish this, elements of the Georgian style were emphasized in various ways—by change of scale, by combinations of features used in ways unknown to the 18th century or simply by repetition. It is such emphasis that helps distinguish the parent from the child. Although the Georgian Revival enjoyed its greatest vogue and most vigorous expression in the last decades of the 19th century and the first of the 20th, it is still a part of the architectural scene. Unfortunately, most modern examples suggest that the creative revival of the Georgian style is a thing of the past. ■

Sandgates on Cat Creek (c. 1740–80), Oakville, Md., is a frame structure with brick ends laid in Flemish bond that shows typically Georgian symmetry. The breakaway chimney, in which the stack is separated from the house for fire protection, is found often in frame houses of the period. (Merry Stinson and Chinh Hoang)

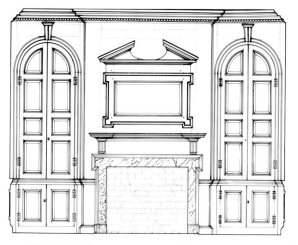

Gunston Hall (c. 1755–59), Lorton, Va., is one of the most important examples of Georgian architecture in America. The east wall of the little parlor has as its focal point a handsome panel with a broken pediment above the mantel. Arched cupboards flank the projecting chimney breast. (Daniel P. Whalen)

Westover (1730), Charles City County,
Va., has a frontispiece styled after Plate
XXVI in Salmon's *Palladio Londinensis*
that seems uneasily attached to a facade with no other strictly ornamental
features. (Thomas T. Waterman)

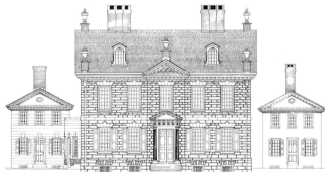

Cliveden (1763–64), Philadelphia, was
one of the finest Georgian country
seats in the American colonies. It
represents a happy compromise between the English Palladian country
house and the Germanic building
tradition. (C. Stanley Runyan and Al-
lan Steenhusen)

The Schley-Rutherford House (1905), Mobile, Ala., has a stairway with typically Georgian balusters. The newel posts, with their reverse tapers and urn finials, however, are unlike anything that would have been found in the 18th century. (Jack E. Boucher)

The McWane House, Lynchburg, Va., has corner pilasters, a hipped roof with balustrades and dormer windows typical of Georgian structures, but the central portico and circular porch pavilions are not Georgian although they are composed of 18th-century elements. The house actually is a mid-19th-century Italianate villa that received its Georgian remodeling about 1910. (HABS collection)

The Wharton-Scott House (1906, Sanguinet and Staats), Fort Worth, Tex., is an exemplary Georgian Revival design. The giant-order portico, gambrel roof, Palladian window and quoins are a few of the identifying elements prominently displayed. (T. E. Stewart).

SPANISH COLONIAL

A third major colonial style flourished in the vast area of southern North America colonized by Spain. Although a number of other European countries, notably France and the Netherlands, established colonies and left architectural legacies in North America, only Spain ranks with England in implanting far-flung and lasting architectural traditions in the United States.

The first permanent Spanish settlement was at St. Augustine, Fla., in 1565. Although some original buildings and fortifications remain there and in scattered locations along the Gulf Coast, the most important concentrations of Spanish colonial architecture are in the mission complexes of the Southwest. The missions were frontier manifestations of the exuberant baroque style of the Spanish Counter-Reformation, especially as it developed in the prosperous colonial centers of Mexico. This style, which dominated North American mission architecture for 200 years, was characterized by twin bell towers, curved gables, sumptuous ornament applied to plain walls, dramatic interior lighting and elaborately carved and painted reredoses.

Frontier priests reproduced the baroque forms with whatever materials and labor were at hand. The New Mexican missions, strongly influenced by Indian building techniques, were the most primitive. These adobe structures usually had massive, unadorned, windowless walls, flat roofs with timbers supported on decorative brackets and clerestory windows to illuminate carved and polychromed altars.

In Texas, Arizona and California, masonry construction and ornamentation by Mexican or European artisans permitted more elaborate although still provincial expression. San Xavier del Bac (1784–97), near Tucson, Ariz., with its complex domes and vaults and ornate entrance portal, represents a high point in architectural development on the Spanish-American frontier.

The secularization of mission lands under Mexican rule in the 1830s encouraged settlement, and the adobe, wood and tile houses that were prevalent through the mid-19th century followed Spanish colonial tradition. All these forms later fell from general use only to be revived in the 1890s. Particularly popular in California, Florida and the Southwest, the Spanish, Pueblo and Mission revival styles drew not only on the provincial forms of missions and haciendas but also on the rounded adobe shapes and projecting timbers of the pueblos and the grand buildings of Mediterranean Spain. ∎

Acoma Pueblo (c. 1300) and its mission church, Casa Blanca, N.M., were built on a rugged landscape typical of many Indian pueblos. (Julsing Lamsam)

San Estevan del Ray Mission Church (c. 1629–42), at Acoma Pueblo, combined native materials, Indian building skills and Spanish baroque forms to produce a uniquely American style. (M. James Slack)

Acoma Pueblo has the flat roofs, projecting vigas and textured adobe of Pueblo Indian construction that appear not only in New Mexico missions but also in 20th-century revival structures. (M. James Slack)

Mission San Xavier del Bac (1784–97), near Tucson, Ariz., is another of the great mission churches erected under the supervision of the Franciscans. As at San Jose, the elaborate central entrance contrasts effectively with the relatively plain surfaces of the flanking towers. (William M. Collier, Jr., and Louis Williams)

Mission San Jose y San Miguel de Aguayo (1720–31), San Antonio, Tex., comes closer to the sophistication of Mexican and Spanish churches than any other Texas mission. The sculptured portal shows the Spanish preference for applying ornate carving to otherwise plain walls. (Fred E. Mang, Jr., National Park Service)

The Don Raimundo Arrivas House (1770–90), St. Augustine, Fla., incorporates portions of Spanish construction dating from about 1725. The first-floor walls are built of coquina, the local limestone composed of broken sea shells. (Jack E. Boucher)

Government Street United Methodist Church (1889–90; 1907, George B. Rogers), Mobile, Ala., is a notable example of the Spanish colonial revival. As with its mission prototypes, the church displays an ornately decorated entrance portal between the relatively plain wall surfaces of the towers. (Jack E. Boucher)

Our Lady of the Wayside Church (1912, Timothy L. Pflueger), Portola Valley, Calif., is a Spanish colonial revival. The architect used the belfry facade of Mission Dolores in nearby San Francisco as his model but added to it a doorway with Georgian motifs. (Jack E. Boucher)

La Jolla Woman's Club (1913–14, Irving J. Gill), La Jolla, Calif., subtly suggests the influence of California's mission architecture in its repeated arches and trellised pergolas. (Marvin Rand)

The Violet Ray (General Petroleum) Gasoline Station (1929), Palo Alto, Calif., reflects Spanish colonial influence in its white stucco surface and low pitched red-tile roofs. (W. Michael Coppa)

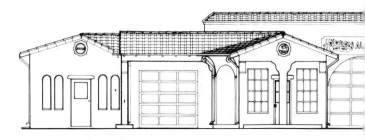

Mar-a-Lago (1923–27, Marion Sims Wyeth), Palm Beach, Fla., represents
Spanish colonial revival at its grandest. Many of its decorative components
were based on Spanish buildings, while others derived from Portuguese and
Venetian motifs. The overall impression, as evidenced in the portal and the
porch, can perhaps best be classified as Mediterranean. (Jack E. Boucher)

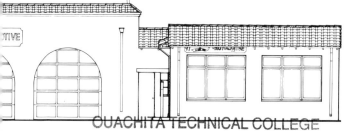

FEDERAL

By 1776 a new style created in Scotland by the Adam
brothers had contended with and overcome Georgian
Palladianism in popularity. The Adamesque style was
essentially a creative amalgam of Renaissance and Palladian
forms, the delicacy of the French rococo and the classical
architecture of Greece and Rome.

This amalgam was chiefly the work of Robert Adam
(1728–92). After a two-year study tour of Italy (including
study of the palace of Roman emperor Diocletian in Split),
Adam in 1764 published the first volume of architectural
measured drawings of domestic Roman architecture. This
and other 18th-century volumes based on archeological
explorations and travel accounts proved that Roman
architecture was richer and more varied than Renaissance
and neo-Palladian architects had acknowledged. Delicate
decorative patterns of urns, swags, sheaths of wheat and
garlands were found on many private homes in Pompeii and
Herculaneum. The plans of houses and palaces, notably
Nero's Golden House in Rome, revealed interior spaces of
hexagonal, oval and circular forms. If the ancients were free
and flexible with plans, proportions and decoration, then
surely, it was thought, late 18th-century architects could
appropriately follow their example.

Although the Revolutionary War ended British reign over
the 13 colonies, it did not terminate the influence of British
architectural styles. Isolated examples of the Adamesque
style had appeared in America before 1776. One of the
earliest examples is the dining room ceiling at Mount
Vernon, which was installed in 1775. Beautifully executed in
plaster, it contains a rinceau border and festoons of husks
surrounding a central rosette. It is significant that one of the

The Dodge-Shreve House (early 19th
century), Salem, Mass., was built with
walls unadorned except for the entrance motif and arched window. Other
Federal features are the shallow hipped
roof and graduated window openings.
(Eric Muller)

first manifestations of the Adamesque style in America is an interior feature, for it was in their decorative interiors that the Adam brothers excelled and differed most pronouncedly from Palladian architectural design.

The Adamesque style as found in the United States is known as the Federal style because it flowered in the early decades of the new nation. Federal-style buildings are found throughout the cities and towns of the eastern seaboard, particularly in New England seaports, where merchant princes were growing rich from their profitable trade. The Federal-style houses they built, in such places as Salem, Mass., and Providence, R.I., were generally square or rectangular, brick or frame, three stories high, topped with low hipped roofs, often with a balustrade. Door and window openings were beautifully scaled and articulated, frequently incorporating fan and oval forms. Columns and moldings were narrow, chaste and delicate compared to the robust features of the earlier Georgian style. In general, exterior decoration was confined to a porch or entrance motif. Interiors differed most noticeably from earlier styles. Rooms were not square or rectangular but oval, circular or octagonal. Mantels, cornices, door and window frames and ceilings were decorated with delicate rosettes, urns, swags and oval patera.

One of the most notable Federal buildings to the south is the Octagon (1799, William Thornton), Washington, D.C., built as the town house of Col. John Tayloe. Its polygonal floor plan and circular and oval rooms illustrate the freedom of expression possible in Federal design. The Nathaniel Russell and William Blacklock houses in Charleston, S.C., both built in the first decade of the 19th century, are also excellent examples of the style. ∎

The Custom House and Public Stores (1818–19), Salem, Mass., shows the Federal style applied to a public building. It has a handsome doorway with an arched window above, but the porch, of the composite order, is more expansive than on domestic examples. (Larry D. Nichols)

Mantel (c. 1815–19), now installed in the S. L. Abbot House, Lynchburg, Va., is a superb example of Federal woodwork. On either side of the firebox opening are triple colonnettes supporting the entablature. (Richard Cheek)

Point of Honor (c. 1815), Lynchburg, Va., an extremely refined example of the Federal style, has doorways with arched fanlights centering the facade on both the first and second levels. The matched polygonal bays on either side of the recessed entrance bays reflect the Federal style's fondness for shapes other than rectangular or square. (Richard Cheek)

The Andrew Ross Tenant Houses (1810–11), Washington, D.C., have simple, well-proportioned facades typical of merchant-class homes of the period. (J. Alexander)

The Jeremiah Sullivan House (1818), Madison, Ind., has a perfect Federal entrance, with a delicate iron railing, glazed fanlight and attenuated three-quarter columns framing the door and sidelights. (Jack E. Boucher)

The Derby Summer House (1794, Samuel McIntyre), Danvers, Mass., is an elegant example of the Federal style. The festoons above the rectangular second-story windows and the urns are typical Federal decorations. Built in Peabody, Mass., the pavilion was moved to Danvers in 1904. (Cervin Robinson)

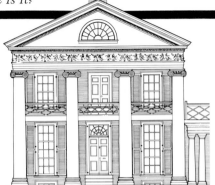

JEFFERSONIAN

Many of the new states built capitols to house their elected officials and to serve as symbols of their new authority and prestige. Virginia asked Thomas Jefferson, then minister to France, to find "an able architect [to design] a plan fit for a Capitol" in its new capital, Richmond. Jefferson did not find an architect—he did the drawings and even prepared a scale model himself. Using as his inspiration the Maison Carrée, a Roman temple at Nîmes in southern France, he created the first pure temple form in American architecture.

In addition to the Virginia State Capitol, Jefferson is remembered for his unique architectural achievement at the University of Virginia in Charlottesville. Here, each of the 10 connected pavilions is different, although each is patterned after a specific Roman or Palladian temple. They were designed to be models "of taste and good architecture," and to "serve as specimens for the architectural lecturer."

Jefferson's pavilion designs—in contrast to the Federal style—were derived from public structures and not from the houses and villas of Roman nobility. Consequently, they have heavy modillions, full-scale cornices and a more masculine feeling than Federal-style mansions. For Thomas Jefferson, the Roman orders were the first principles of architecture and symbolized the republican form of government he believed was being revived in the New World.

Many red-brick houses and courthouses that derive from Jefferson's architectural theories are found in Virginia and states where Virginians settled. They could be termed Roman Revival, but it is perhaps more fitting to call them Jeffersonian. Until the name of architect Henry Hobson Richardson was unalterably wedded to the Romanesque in the late 19th century, no architectural style was so closely identified with one American. ∎

The Main Hotel Building (1830s), Old Sweet Springs, W. Va., has unfluted columns, red-brick walls with white trim and fanlights, all reminiscent of Jefferson's University of Virginia. (Richard Cheek)

Pavilion II, University of Virginia (1822, Thomas Jefferson), Charlottesville, Va., was adapted from the ancient Roman temple of Fortuna Virilis, familiar to Jefferson from the drawings of Palladio. The red-brick walls and louvered shutters, however, are pure Virginia. (Michael D. Sullivan)

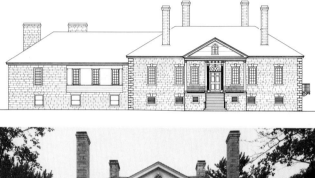

Belle Grove (c. 1795), Middletown, Va., resembles other houses influenced by Jefferson that were often one story on a raised basement with a small Roman portico. In this instance, Jefferson himself gave "the favor of [his] advice on the Plan." The formal symmetry of the facade is compromised by the side wing, which was added sometime between 1815 and 1820. (Rebecca Rogers; Jack E. Boucher)

GREEK REVIVAL

Although Jefferson favored the Roman mode, one of his younger contemporaries was sufficiently sure of himself to declare without reservation that his "principles of good taste . . . [were] rigid in Grecian Architecture." Benjamin Henry Latrobe (1764–1820), an architect and engineer who was responsible for some of America's most notable structures, was born in England and educated on the Continent. He emigrated to the United States in 1796 and by 1798 had designed the Bank of Pennsylvania in Philadelphia, the first American building to incorporate a classical Greek order, the Ionic.

Many Greek Revival structures were built in Europe and its colonies, but in the United States during the 1830s and 1840s the style flourished as nowhere else. One reason for its appeal here undoubtedly was the often expressed sentiment that America, with its democratic ideals, was the spiritual successor of ancient Greece, a feeling evident not only in the architecture but also in the very names of newly established towns—Athens, Sparta, Ithaca—from Georgia to Maine and throughout the Midwest. In 1842 architect Alexander Jackson Davis complained that it was difficult for strangers in American towns "to distinguish between a church, a bank and a hall of justice." He might have included houses as well, for by this time the Greek temple-front building was so prevalent that it was used for all these functions and others as well.

The most easily identified features of a Greek-inspired building are columns and pilasters, although not every Greek Revival structure has them. Other hallmarks of the style are bold, simple moldings on both the exterior and the interior, pedimented gables, heavy cornices with unadorned friezes and horizontal transoms above entrances. Ancient Greek structures did not use arches; consequently, with the rise of the Greek Revival the arched entrances and fan windows so common in the Federal and Jeffersonian styles were abandoned. Most Greek Revival frame houses were painted white because it was not then known that the white marble of ancient Greek buildings had often been polychromed.

Although the style was fostered by handbooks and plan books for carpenters, as were earlier architectural developments in America, the Greek Revival also inspired the nation's first great professional architects. Among those who designed in the style were Benjamin Henry Latrobe, William Strickland, Asher Benjamin and Thomas U. Walter. ■

Andalusia (c. 1797, 1834, Thomas U. Walter), near Philadelphia, is one of the most noted Greek Revival houses in America. To an existing earlier house, Walter made additions for owner Nicholas Biddle and crowned his work with this impressive Doric portico. (Jack E. Boucher)

The Governor's Mansion (1853–55, Abner Cook), Austin, Tex., is a graceful Greek Revival structure that has a six-column Ionic portico sheltering a second-floor balcony, as well as a full entablature concealing a low hipped roof. (Jack E. Boucher)

The Brown-Augustine House (c. 1834), near New Carlisle, Ind., is a classic Greek Revival example as interpreted in the old Northwest Territory. Flanking the temple front, with its pedimented portico, are one-story wings. (E. J. Wieczorek)

Engine Company No. 3 (1853), Sacramento, Calif., has a flat roof behind its imposing Greek Revival pediment, belying the temple design suggested by the facade. (Glen Fishback)

The Costigan House (1850–52, Francis Costigan), Madison, Ind., shows the architect-owner's mastery of Greek form and proportion, particularly in the relation of the porch entablature to the main one. (Jack E. Boucher)

The Old Patent Office (1836–67, William P. Elliott and Robert Mills), Washington, D.C., has a south portico copied directly from the Parthenon. The building now houses two Smithsonian Institution museums. (Jack E. Boucher)

The Brues House (c. 1853), Wheeling,
W. Va., has a Greek Revival portico that
provides a miniature temple front to
the house. Not content with this
embellishment alone, the builder also
framed the dormer windows above
with pilasters and pediments. (Jack E.
Boucher)

The William F. Kuehneman House, Racine, Wis., is in the popular temple form,
which replaced the log cabin as a common Midwest house type in the 1840s
and 1850s. Greek Revival features include fluted Doric columns, flat corner
pilasters, a wide, plain frieze and a horizontal transom over the door. (Cervin
Robinson)

GOTHIC REVIVAL

In the late 18th and early 19th centuries, styles in literature, art and architecture rapidly changed in both Europe and the United States. One of the more pervasive currents was the romantic movement, which proclaimed the superiority of the Christian medieval past. With almost religious fervor romantics extolled the symbolic virtues of Gothic architecture and fostered its revival.

Gothic Revival architecture came to America from England; however, it never achieved widespread popularity here, perhaps because of its strong association with Britain, liturgical Christianity and aristocracy—all suspect to the New World "democrat." The first American residence to employ Gothic details was Sedgeley (1799, Benjamin Henry Latrobe), a country house outside Philadelphia. In the first quarter of the 19th century, other major architects also experimented with the Gothic Revival style, usually in the design of country mansions and churches, occasionally in public buildings and prisons.

By the 1830s a growing taste for the romantic, fostered largely by the novels of Sir Walter Scott, and dissatisfaction with the restraints of classical architecture turned the Gothic Revival into a popular movement. Alexander Jackson Davis was the country's most prolific Gothic Revival architect. His plans for houses and cottages were widely distributed in the popular books of Andrew Jackson Downing, pioneer landscape architect and arbiter of midcentury taste. The picturesque country cottages advocated by Davis and Downing dotted the countryside in the 1840s and 1850s and continued to be built in some areas long after the Civil War.

Gothic Revival was distinguished by the pointed arch, which could ingeniously be combined with towers, crenellation, steep gabled roofs, lacy bargeboards, verandas, clustered columns, foliated ornaments, bay and oriel windows, tracery and leaded stained glass. House plans were asymmetrical to allow flexibility in arrangement of rooms and create picturesque external silhouettes. The timely invention of the scroll saw, or jigsaw, and the widespread availability of wood also produced that delightful national adaptation known as Carpenter Gothic. More elaborate masonry houses, such as Alexander Jackson Davis's masterpiece, Lyndhurst (1838, 1864–65), a National Trust property near Tarrytown, N.Y., aspired to greater Gothic authenticity.

Lacking models, domestic Gothic structures never achieved the correctness of mid-19th-century churches. American church architects were strongly influenced by Augustus W. N. Pugin and the English ecclesiologists who vigorously promoted the archeologically accurate Gothic parish church as the only suitable structure for Christian worship.

The Gothic Revival was an enduring style. Post–Civil War Gothic Revivalists were influenced by the writings of English architecture theorist John Ruskin, who advocated the use of contrasting colors of brick and stone to produce bold polychromatic patterns. The Ruskinian, or High Victorian Gothic, style was eclectic, drawing on Italian and German as well as English Gothic precedents. The style was used mainly for public buildings, including schools, libraries and churches. Such highly personalized work as that of Philadelphia architect Frank Furness reveals the extent to

The First Baptist Church (1884–86, John R. Thomas), Lynchburg, Va., is an authoritative statement of the High Victorian Gothic style. The rose window centering the gabled facade is one of three lighting the sanctuary. (Richard Cheek)

The William J. Rotch House (1846, A. J. Davis and William R. Emerson), New Bedford, Mass., is one of the Gothic villas designed by Davis that was illustrated in the works of A. J. Downing, where it was entitled "A Cottage-Villa in the Rural Gothic Style." (Ned Goode)

which Gothic forms were adapted to post–Civil War tastes.

Reacting to the excesses of High Victorian Gothic, late 19th-century architects returned to a more imitative Gothic Revival. The Collegiate Gothic that shaped such campuses as Princeton University and the University of Pennsylvania was popular in this period. Gothic also remained the most influential style for churches well into the 20th century. ■

The Old State Capitol (1847–49, James H. Dakin; reconstructed 1880–82, William A. Freret), Baton Rouge, La., is one of only two antebellum Gothic state capitols, a style seldom used for government buildings. (David J. Kaminsky)

Lyndhurst (1838, 1864–65, A. J. Davis),
Tarrytown, N.Y., is an elaborate,
castlelike Gothic Revival house.
Picturesque asymmetry, a variety of
foliated windows, battlements, towers,
finials, stone, tracery and ample
verandas can all be seen in this
National Trust property. (Jack E.
Boucher; Lawrence J. Fusaro and Roger
Erickson)

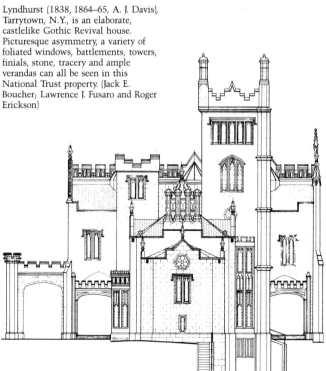

The Bowen House (c. 1845, Joseph C. Wells), Woodstock, Conn., shows the felicitous combination of Gothic design with frame construction. Board-and-batten siding, seen here, was often employed to give the desired sense of verticality. Even the fence surrounding the yard carries the Gothic theme. (Jack E. Boucher)

Chapel Hall, Gallaudet College (1867–70, Frederick C. Withers), Washington, D.C., is one of the earliest examples of Ruskinian Gothic collegiate architecture in the U.S. Withers continued his Ruskinian Gothic design in the arcaded corridor connecting Chapel Hall (the main building at Gallaudet) with College Hall, built 1875–78. (Ronald Comedy)

Rochester Free Academy (1872–73, A. J. Warner), Rochester, N.Y., illustrates the principles of Ruskinian Gothic. Two kinds of stone trim are set against red-brick walls for a polychromatic effect. Gothic details in windows, doors and gables are large scale. (Hans Padelt)

The Syracuse Savings Bank (1875, Joseph Lyman Silsbee), Syracuse, N.Y., shows the effective use of contrasts in color and texture as promulgated by Ruskin. (Jack E. Boucher)

The Provident Life and Trust Company (1876-79, Frank Furness), Philadelphia, was obviously an original work but owed a debt to the High Victorian Gothic. (Theodore F. Dillon)

ITALIANATE

The architecture of Italy inspired the building style that enjoyed immense popularity in the 10 years before the Civil War. Also known as the Tuscan, Lombard, Round, Bracketed and even the American style, the Italianate could be as picturesque as the Gothic or as restrained as the classical. This adaptability made it nearly a national style in the 1850s.

Italianate villa design was borrowed from the rural architecture of northern Italy and introduced by way of England in the late 1830s. Again, it was the plans of Alexander Jackson Davis circulated in Andrew Jackson Downing's books that helped popularize the style.

At its most elaborate, the Italianate house had a low roof, overhanging eaves with decorative brackets, an entrance

The Patrick Barry House (1857, Gervase Wheeler), Rochester, N.Y., is representative of the full-blown Italian villa style. Advancing and receding planes, arched window heads, shallow gabled-roof sections supported by a bracketed cornice and a tower characterize the type. Wheeler, like Downing and Davis, helped promulgate the villa style in works such as his *Rural Homes* (1853). (Hans Padelt)

The Benjamin Harrison House (1874-76, H. Brandt), Indianapolis, features windows, alternating with blind panels between the brackets in the frieze, that light a third-floor ballroom. The one-story Ionic porch is an early 20th-century addition. (Ronald J. Lake)

tower, round-headed windows with hood moldings, corner quoins, arcaded porches and balustraded balconies. At its simplest, it was a square house with low pyramidal roof, bracketed eaves and perhaps a cupola or lantern. Both the round-headed windows of Tuscan villas and the classical architraves of Renaissance palaces frequently were used to ornament the facades of urban row houses and commercial buildings.

The development of cast iron and pressed metal technology in the mid-19th century permitted the economical mass production of decorative features that few merchants could have afforded in carved stone. New York City, St. Louis and Portland, Ore., all had districts of cast-iron buildings, and towns across the country still boast stores with cast-iron fronts masquerading as Italian palaces. ■

The Main House, James Lick Mill complex (c. 1860), Santa Clara, Calif., is a good example of the Italianate style adapted in wood to a domestic structure. (Jane Lidz)

The Chalfonte Hotel (1875–76, 1879), Cape May, N.J., demonstrates the adaptability of the Italianate to another building type—the summer resort hotel. The Chalfonte is only one of many examples of the style that grace one of America's foremost Victorian towns. (Jack E. Boucher)

The Reed Building (1885), Wheeling, W. Va., has elaborate second-story window lintels, executed in wood rather than cast iron, and an extremely ornate cornice. (Jack E. Boucher)

First National Bank Building (1877, P. M. Comegys), Galveston, Tex., is typical of Italianate commercial buildings. The first-floor facade is of cast iron, the second of brick. Capping the building is the requisite heavy, bracketed cornice. (Allen Stross)

The Hart (Hildebrand) Block (1884, Charles D. Meyer), Louisville, Ky., possesses a cast-iron facade that reflects classical treatment. All five floors have slender columns with modified Corinthian capitals. (C. Alexander; Jack E. Boucher)

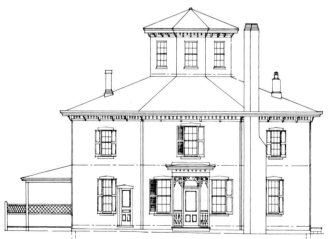

The Bebb (Octagonal) House (1865), Washington, D.C., shows a house type that flourished in the mid-19th century after the publication of Orson Squire Fowler's *A Home for All*, which claimed that the octagon was a far more efficient and space-saving shape for a house than the usual square or rectangle. The unusual form was often embellished with Italianate details. (HABS collection)

EXOTIC REVIVALS

Architects in the 19th century explored exotic historic styles in their search for appropriate symbolism.

French archeological work in Egypt under Napoleon focused attention on Egyptian forms. The massive ancient Egyptian monuments connoted permanence, a quality reflected in the relatively few structures built in the United States in the Egyptian Revival style. They include prisons, mausoleums, cemetery gates, churches and monuments. The obelisk was thought to be particularly appropriate for public memorials. Even George Washington was commemorated with this Egyptian form in the Washington Monument (1848–85, Robert Mills).

Although many 19th-century houses had fashionable "Turkish corners," the use of Near Eastern architectural motifs was rare. A few grand and generally ostentatious mansions, such as P. T. Barnum's Bridgeport, Conn., mansion, Iranistan (1847–48), which burned in 1857, sprouted bulbous domes and horseshoe arches, but the Moorish style was most popular for garden structures and such "pleasure palaces" as clubs, hotels and theaters. For quite different reasons, the Moorish Revival also became associated with the Jewish reform movement in America; it distinguished synagogues from churches and had historical precedent in the beautiful Mudejar synagogues of Spain that were built before the 15th century.

On the eve of the Civil War, the United States was a country of diverse interests, cultures and tastes. Nowhere was this diversity seen so clearly as in its architecture, and if the latter half of the 19th century is remembered as the period in which many styles battled for prominence, the seeds of that architectural conflict had already been sown by midcentury. ■

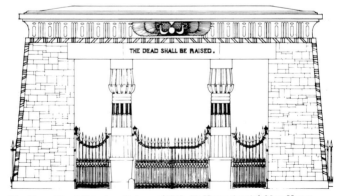

The Grove Street Cemetery Entrance (1845–48, Henry Austin), New Haven, Conn., is an outstanding example of Egyptian Revival architecture of monumental proportions. (A. H. M. Gottschalk)

The Isaac M. Wise Temple (1863–65, James Keyes Wilson), Cincinnati, used characteristically intricate surface ornament and minaretlike spires to achieve a Moorish Revival flavor.

The First (Downtown) Presbyterian Church (1849–51, William Strickland), Nashville, has the battered window and door frames, concave cornice, winged-disk motif, reeded columns with horizontal bands and palm capitals that appeared on many such Egyptian Revival buildings. (Jack E. Boucher)

The Ada Theater (1926-27, Frederick C. Hummel), Boise, Idaho, opened under the name Egyptian Theatre. The huge columns flanking the organ screen were designed after those in Karnak. (Duane Garrett)

Debtors' Wing of the Philadelphia County (Moyamensing) Prison (1836, Thomas U. Walter), Philadelphia, is considered the first archeologically based Egyptian Revival building in the U.S. (Jack E. Boucher)

SECOND EMPIRE

The popularity of the Second Empire style in the 1860s and 1870s reflects the public interest in picturesqueness and asymmetry, characteristics introduced to American architecture by the Gothic Revival and Italianate styles that became even more pronounced in the mid- to late 19th century. Architecture of this period, although still usually based on historical precedent, represented a reaction to the historical bent of the earlier revivalists. Midcentury architects reasoned that no age had produced the perfect architectural expression and that they could benefit from all the best of the past. Why hesitate, therefore, to combine features from various styles? Freer adaptation could evoke the spirit of the past without slavish imitation and would allow more creativity. Thus, eclecticism characterized much of the architecture of the immediate post–Civil War period, as did a continued emphasis on the picturesque. Great importance was placed on character and a sense of permanence in buildings. "Delicate" and "beautiful" are adjectives rarely used in describing post–Civil War architecture.

The Second Empire style was borrowed from France. It is named for the reign of Napoleon III (1852–70), who undertook a major building campaign that transformed Paris into a city of grand boulevards and monumental buildings that were copied throughout Europe and the New World. One of Napoleon's most famous projects was the enlargement of the Louvre (1852–57), which brought back to popularity a roof form developed by 17th-century French Renaissance architect François Mansart.

The mansard roof—a double-pitched roof with a steep lower slope—was a hallmark of the Second Empire style. By increasing head room in the attic space, it provided an additional usable floor. To provide light on this floor, the mansard roof was almost always pierced with dormers. One of the first major Second Empire–style buildings in America was the Corcoran Gallery (1859–61, James Renwick), Washington, D.C. Confiscated for military use when the Civil War began, the building (now the Renwick Gallery) set the style for many post–Civil War public buildings. In fact, the style became so closely associated with public architecture of the prosperous Grant administration that it is sometimes called the General Grant Style.

Second Empire buildings featured prominent projecting and receding surfaces often in the form of central and end pavilions. Ornamentation usually included classical pediments (often with sculpture groups), balustrades and windows flanked by columns or pilasters. Columns were usually paired and supported entablatures that divided the floors of the building. And there was always the mansard roof. The general effect was monumental and ornate and provided comfortable associations with the latest European building fashion.

Domestic architecture in the Second Empire style is more difficult to characterize because the mansard roof could be placed on almost any house to create a contemporary look without requiring innovations in plan or ornament. The interiors were generally elaborations of the Italianate style, with bold plaster cornices and medallions and marble fireplaces with arched openings.

Although a house with a mansard roof can safely be termed Second Empire regardless of what decorative

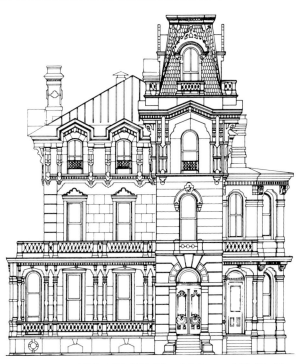

The Goyer-Lee House (1843, 1853, 1873, Edward C. Jones and Mathias H. Baldwin), Memphis, Tenn., is an authoritative statement of the Second Empire style. The brick facade is covered with sandstone veneer and stucco, making it appear more monumental. (Mark P. Frederickson and Darrell K. Pattison)

elements may ornament its facade, other domestic styles in the third quarter of the 19th century—with the exception of the Romanesque Revival—are not so easily distinguished. Many architectural historians lump them together under the term "picturesque eclecticism," and writer John Maass has called it the "nameless period." Domestic architecture of this period freely mixed elements from several styles, and it is sometimes difficult to pinpoint the borrowings. ■

The Capt. Edward Penniman House (1867–68), Eastham, Mass., proves that even a small, square, one-story house could appear grand with the imaginative addition of a mansard roof. (Cervin Robinson)

Terrace Hill (1867–69, W. W. Boyington), Des Moines, Iowa, is one of the most lavish Second Empire houses in the country. The concrete quoins and window hoods contrast with the red-brick walls. The house now serves as the Iowa Governor's Mansion. (Robert Thall)

The State, War and Navy (Old Executive Office) Building (1871–88, Alfred B. Mullett), Washington, D.C., is one of the two grandest American public buildings in the Second Empire style; the other is Philadelphia City Hall (1871, John McArthur, Jr.). The State, War and Navy Building has projecting pavilions with superimposed columns, classical pediments and balustrades and a massive mansard roof with two rows of decorative dormers. (Ronald Comedy)

The 2300 block of Chapline Street in Wheeling, W. Va., contains several good examples of the Second Empire style in an urban setting. Similar massing, window spacing and unified cornice lines contribute to the homogeneous grouping. (Mark L. Hall, Ed Freeman and Richard Cronenberger)

STICK STYLE

Evolving out of the Carpenter Gothic, the Stick Style flourished in the mid-19th century. This style of wood construction was characterized by angularity, verticality and asymmetry. Roofs were composed of steep intersecting gables. Verandas and porches were common and were often decorated with simple diagonal braces.

In keeping with the idea that architecture should be truthful, the principal characteristic of the Stick Style was the expression of the inner structure of the house through the exterior ornament. Most often found on gable ends and upper stories, this stick work was usually a series of boards intersecting at right angles and applied over the clapboard surface to symbolize the structural skeleton. Sometimes diagonal boards were incorporated to resemble half-timbering. ■

The Griswold House (1862–63, Richard Morris Hunt), Newport, R.I., is an elaborate example of the Stick Style. Intersecting boards are superimposed on the clapboard sheathing to suggest the interior framing. All trim is simple and angular. (Jack E. Boucher)

The Dr. Emlen Physick House (1879, Frank Furness), Cape May, N.J., is designed in the Stick Style. The bold design, tapering chimneys, steeply hipped roofs, tall proportions, structural framing overlay and irregular silhouette are typical of Furness's work. (Hugh McCauley)

The David King House (1871-72), Newport, R.I., has diagonal braces and exposed Stick Style framing. The porch, however, is attached to a mansard-roof house, illustrating how styles were mixed in the post–Civil War period. (Jack E. Boucher)

QUEEN ANNE

The very name of this style suggested eclecticism to its originators. It was coined in England to describe buildings that supposedly were inspired by the transitional architecture of the pre-Georgian period when classical ornament was grafted onto buildings of basically medieval form. The English architect most closely associated with the Queen Anne style was Richard Norman Shaw (1831–1912), whose sprawling manor houses were well known to American architects.

The Queen Anne style played on contrast of materials. First floors were often brick or stone; upper stories were of stucco, clapboard or decorative shingles, which were used frequently in the United States in place of the tiles popular in England. Huge medieval-type chimneys were common. Roofs were gabled or hipped, often with second-story projections and corner turrets borrowed from French châteaux. Gable ends were ornamented with half-timbering or stylized relief decoration. Molded or specially shaped bricks were used as decorative accents. Banks of casement windows were common, and upper panes were often outlined with stained-glass squares. Verandas and balconies opened houses to the outdoors.

Interior plans, which had been moving further and further from classical symmetry, were given even greater freedom. The fully developed Queen Anne plan featured the living hall, a central living and circulation space with both

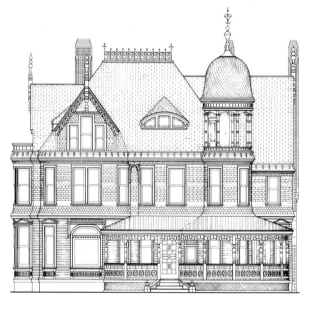

The Long-Waterman House (1889, D. B. Benson), San Diego, Calif., is an all-wood version of the Queen Anne style. Contrast is achieved between the narrow first-floor clapboards and the intricate second-floor shingle patterns. Gables are steep; turrets also provide vertical accents. The encircling veranda has spindlelike ornaments often found on the interior and exterior of Queen Anne houses. (J. Livengood; City of San Diego)

The Ivinson Mansion (1892), Laramie, Wyo., with its verticality, projecting gables, prominent porch, corner bays and turrets, has common Queen Anne features. (Jack E. Boucher)

Glenmont (1880, Henry Hudson Holly), West Orange, N.J., the home of Thomas Edison, shows such Queen Anne characteristics as a brick first story contrasted with decorative boarding on the second story, shingles in the gables, a paneled chimney and prominent gables. (Jack E. Boucher)

The Col. Walter Gresham House (The Bishop's Palace) (1887–93, Nicholas J. Clayton), Galveston, Tex., has an elaborate tile roof with hips, gables, cones and pyramids corresponding to the articulation of the complex asymmetrical plan. The stonework relates the house to the Richardsonian Romanesque. (Allen Stross)

fireplace and grand staircase. This space flowed freely into other ample rooms. Rich, dark woods in wall paneling and beamed ceilings replaced the plaster ornament and bright wallpapers of the Italianate and Second Empire styles.

The first true American Queen Anne building was architect H. H. Richardson's William Watts Sherman House (1874) in Newport, R.I. The informality and amplitude of the Queen Anne were perfect for the summer "cottages" of Newport, but the style—especially with its prominent corner turrets—was also the choice of bankers and physicians in small-town America until the turn of the century. The Queen Anne also changed urban row-house architecture. The projecting bay front topped by a gable or pinnacle roof was found in cities from Boston to San Francisco in the 1880s. Decorative brick patterns, molded bricks and colorful stained-glass transoms enlivened the face of the row house. Similar features were found in small commercial buildings of the 1880s and 1890s, but the picturesque effects of the Queen Anne style were employed to best advantage in substantial, free-standing residences. ■

SHINGLE STYLE

An American style that evolved out of the Queen Anne was the Shingle Style. It was born in New England, where the fondness for natural wood shingles reflected post-Centennial interest in American colonial architecture, especially the shingle architecture of the coastal towns that were being rediscovered as fashionable resorts. The reappearance of the gambrel roof in some Shingle Style structures was also a result of this antiquarian interest.

Although many Shingle Style buildings fall somewhere along the line of evolution from the Queen Anne, the first examples of the fully developed style appeared in the 1880s. Among the important practitioners of the style were architects Willis Polk in the West and H. H. Richardson, Bruce Price, William Ralph Emerson, John Calvin Stevens and McKim, Mead and White in the East.

Shingle Style buildings were tamer and more horizontal than their Queen Anne predecessors. Roofs continued to be prominent and complex, but dormers were often hipped or eyebrow rather than gabled. Ornament was reduced. Circular turrets and verandas remained popular but were integrated more fully into the overall design. Most important, the entire building was usually covered with wooden shingles. When a contrasting material was used, as for porch columns and foundations, it was often rough-surfaced, coursed stone or fieldstone rubble, which complemented the rough natural texture of the shingles. The emphasis of the Shingle Style was on the surface—the shingle covering that unified all parts of the building. The interior plan continued the Queen Anne trend toward openness and informality. ■

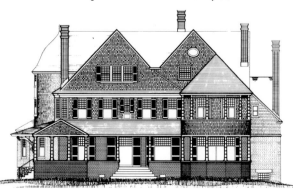

The William G. Low House (1887, McKim, Mead and White), Bristol, R.I., was one of the great Shingle Style monuments. A myriad of window forms, an ample veranda and projecting bays were all controlled by the simple roof and the shingle covering. (Cervin Robinson)

The Sea Cliff Inn (1886), Nantucket, Mass., was a typical Shingle Style hotel, a style closely associated with northeastern resort architecture. Both the shingle covering and the Palladian windows in the gables indicated renewed interest in American colonial architecture. (Jack E. Boucher)

The Isaac Bell House (Edna Villa) (1882–83, McKim, Mead and White), Newport, R.I., has a relatively calm silhouette and a distinctive horizontal massing. The shingle covering unifies the somewhat disparate massing of the windows. (Thomas B. Schubert)

RICHARDSONIAN ROMANESQUE

In only a few instances has an American architectural style been so influenced by one figure as to bear that person's name. But so it was with Henry Hobson Richardson (1838–86) and the late 19th-century Romanesque Revival.

American architects had experimented with the Romanesque in the 1840s and 1850s for churches and public buildings, using round arches, corbels and historically correct features such as chevrons and lozenges borrowed from the pre-Gothic architecture of Europe. But in texture and outline these early Romanesque structures resembled their Gothic Revival contemporaries. The outstanding example of this early phase of the style is the original Smithsonian Institution building (1847–55, James Renwick), Washington, D.C. It was designed with extremely irregular outlines, battlemented cornices and relatively smooth-faced ashlar walls.

As interpreted by Richardson in the 1870s and 1880s, the Romanesque became a different, and uniquely American, style. Still present were the round arches framing window and door openings, but gone were vertical silhouettes and smooth stone facings. Richardson's buildings were more horizontal and rough in texture. Heaviness was an ever-present characteristic of the style—emphasized not only by the stone construction but also by deep window reveals, cavernous door openings and, occasionally, bands of

The John J. Glessner House (1885–87, H. H. Richardson), Chicago, is one of the architect's finest houses. It shows simple massing and inherent patterns of coursed masonry used effectively for ornamental effect. (Eric N. Delony; Cervin Robinson)

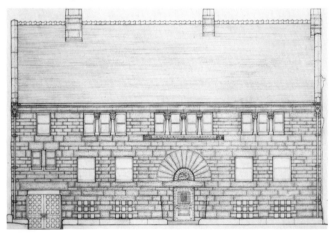

Union Station (1900), Nashville, indicates the style's long popularity. The building's debt to Richardson is obvious in the rock-faced masonry, round arches, soaring tower and general massiveness. (Jack E. Boucher)

The Inner Quad Arcade (1891, Shepley, Rutan and Coolidge), Stanford University, Stanford, Calif., combines Richardsonian masonry with a rhythmic arcade suggestive of the California missions. The complex was designed by the successor firm to Richardson's and succeeded in accomplishing the donor's request that the buildings have a distinctly California flavor. (Jack E. Boucher)

Wayne County Court House
(1890–93, James McLaughlin),
Richmond, Ind., is a good example of
the many Richardsonian Romanesque
courthouses built throughout the
country in the late 19th century.
Their powerful masonry masses
suggest the majesty of the law. The
recessed loggia above the entrance
gives a touch of relief from the heavy
masonry facade and allowed the
stonemasons a chance to display
their talents. (Jack E. Boucher)

Riley Row (1887, Wilcox and
Johnston), St. Paul, Minn., has the
rough stone trim, squat columns and
arched openings found on many late
19th-century Richardsonian
Romanesque row houses. (Jack E.
Boucher)

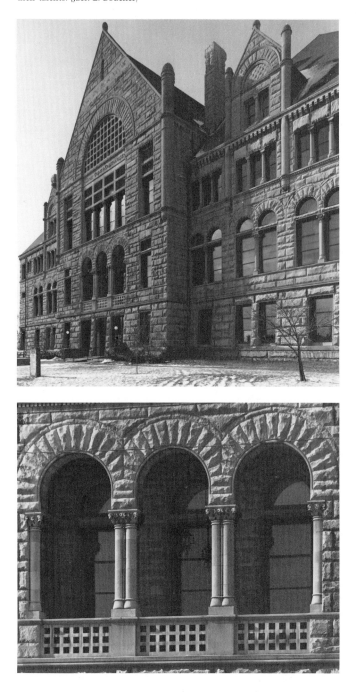

windows. These openings were often further defined by a contrasting color or texture of stone or by short, robust columns. Richardsonian Romanesque was favored for churches, university buildings and public buildings such as railroad stations and courthouses. Consequently, towers were often part of the design. In the best examples, a single tower, massive and bold in outline, crowns the ensemble.

Just as one architect was responsible for this style, one building established its popularity. Richardson's 1872 design for Trinity Church in Boston won one of the most prestigious architectural competitions of the day. Although it is more revivalistic than some of his later structures, Trinity Church has a massiveness and disposition of parts that is uniquely Richardsonian. Others of his designs, such as Pittsburgh's Allegheny County Courthouse and Jail (1884–88), had perhaps even more influence. In countless West Virginia towns downstream from Pittsburgh, as well as in states farther west, county courthouses can be found that are patterned after this building. Especially after Richardson's premature death in 1886, admiring architects adopted his style for schools, post offices and commercial and federal buildings across the country.

Although Richardson produced fewer houses in the Romanesque style (he is also noted for his Queen Anne and Shingle Style designs), there were enough to inspire a plethora of followers. A large house was required to support the massive stoniness of the Romanesque style, but elements of Richardson's work—such as broad round arches, squat columns, eyebrow dormers and carved, intertwining floral details—found their way into the vocabulary of many local builders. Numerous masonry row houses still exist to pay tribute to Richardson's creativity and immense popularity. ■

BEAUX-ARTS

Les beaux-arts—the fine arts—refers essentially to the
aesthetic principles enunciated and perpetuated by the Ecole
des Beaux-Arts in France. The Ecole was established in the
Napoleonic era as the successor to that part of the French
Académie that was founded in the 17th century to monitor
painting, sculpture and architecture. The doctrines and
teaching techniques of the Ecole dominated French
architecture until the 20th century. Therefore, the Beaux-
Arts tradition spans a period of more than 250 years and
includes designs as diverse as the officially sanctioned east
facade of the Louvre (1667–70) and the Paris Opéra (1861–74).
Stylistically, it is almost impossible to use the same words to
describe the calm, horizontal, elegant, rhythmic Louvre east
facade and the exuberant, wedding-cake Opéra. The latter,
more than any other French structure, epitomizes the Second
Empire style and exemplifies the *horror vacui*—an
abhorrence of undecorated surface areas—that is
characteristic of one phase of the Beaux-Arts tradition.

The American architects who were trained in Paris at the
Ecole or by other American architects who had studied there
are legion. Starting with Richard Morris Hunt, who in 1846
was the first American to attend the Ecole, a partial list
includes Louis Sullivan, H. H. Richardson, John Stewardson,
Bernard Maybeck, Addison Mizner, Julia Morgan, John
Mervin Carrère and Thomas Hastings. All were influenced
by the academic design principles of the Ecole, which
emphasized the study of Greek and Roman structures,
composition, symmetry and elaborate two-dimensional wash
or watercolor renderings of the buildings.

Because of their idealized origins, the American Beaux-
Arts designs generally were colossal public buildings. This
phase of the Beaux-Arts tradition is represented in the
United States by the exuberant design for Memorial Hall
(1875–76, Hermann J. Schwarzmann) at the Centennial
Exposition in Philadelphia and by Grand Central Terminal
(1903–13, Reed and Stem; Warren and Wetmore) in New
York City.

Near the end of the century, however, such designs—with
their heavy ashlar stone bases, grand stairways, paired
columns with plinths, monumental attics, grand arched
openings, cartouches, decorative swags, medallions and
sculptural figures—gave way to more sedate forms, which
were used for the town houses and the country and resort
villas of the rich. ∎

The Tremaine-Gallagher House (c. 1914, F. W. Striebinger), Cleveland Heights, Ohio, is a domestic-scale example of the late Beaux-Arts style, which was characterized by a quiet elegance suited to a large suburban mansion such as this. (Martin Linsey)

Whitehall (1900–02, Carrère and Hastings), Palm Beach, Fla., has a monumental main stair whose bronze balustrade is perfectly complemented by the ornate furnishings. (Jack E. Boucher)

The A. C. Bliss House (1907, A. Goenner), Washington, D.C., proves that the Beaux-Arts style was an amalgam—here mixing Roman quoins, an oversized late Renaissance dormer with a broken pediment and an exaggerated, steep roof that shows French late medieval influence. (Jack E. Boucher)

The Library of Congress (1889–97, Smithmeyer and Pelz), Washington, D.C., is one of America's most grandiose Beaux-Arts designs. Nearly every element of the style is found here, including the monumental entrance stairway. (Jack E. Boucher)

The City of Paris Dry Goods Company (1896, Clinton Day; reconstructed 1908–09, James R. Miller), San Francisco, was an early Beaux-Arts commercial structure in San Francisco. This detail shows an Art Nouveau influence appropriate to its name. (Robert Freed)

CLASSICAL REVIVAL

The later, more refined stage of the Beaux-Arts tradition
influenced the last phase of the classical revival in the
United States. Federal government buildings of the first half
of the 20th century owed much to the Beaux-Arts
interpretation of classical design. The Cannon Office
Building (1908, Carrère and Hastings) of the House of
Representatives, with its calm composition of giant paired
columns on an ashlar base and arched fenestration, is a
reflection of Perrault's design for the east facade of the
Louvre. No matter how Roman the Jefferson Memorial
(1937–43) may appear at first sight, the fact that its architect,
John Russell Pope, studied at the Ecole (as did Carrère and
Hastings) suggests that the 20th-century classical revival in
the United States was the child more of the Beaux-Arts
tradition than of the ancient Mediterranean world.

In the late 19th and early 20th centuries, commissions for
public buildings and grand houses of industrial moguls went
to architects trained in the Beaux-Arts tradition. These
architects generally produced academic designs based on
classical or Renaissance precedents.

The tradition of academic revivals also included Gothic,
Tudor, Georgian and Spanish colonial styles, all of which
enjoyed great popularity from the 1890s through the 1920s.
During this same period, however, structures were built that
were not inspired by styles of the past. It was these
structures, rather than their more popular contemporaries,
that heralded the course of 20th-century architecture. ■

The Cannon House Office Building (1908, Carrère and Hastings), Washington,
D.C., with its monumental size, grand entrance stairs, rusticated podium and
arched first-floor windows, typifies the late classical revival style, which was
especially popular for government buildings and monuments, particularly in
the nation's capital. (Jack E. Boucher)

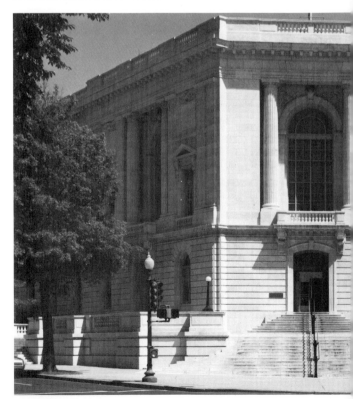

Lynchburg National Bank (1915-16, Alfred C. Bossom), Lynchburg, Va., shows the careful attention paid to the siting of classical revival buildings. Both elevations of this corner building are important and, while obviously related to each other, are subtly different. (Richard Cheek)

CHICAGO SCHOOL

Chicago is the site associated with development of the tall
commercial building. Although Chicago commercial
architecture built on advances made elsewhere, most notably
in Philadelphia and New York City, it was in that
midwestern city in the last quarter of the 19th century that
new technology and materials were exploited by innovative
architects and engineers to produce the skeleton-framed
skyscraper that would transform cities around the world.

The commercial architecture of the Chicago School was
the result of important advances in construction technology.
Building height had been limited by the massiveness of the
masonry walls needed for support, even after invention of
the passenger elevator made upper stories easily accessible.
Numerous architects experimented with the use of cast- and
wrought-iron members to carry the weight of interior floors,
but it was not until construction of the Home Life Building
(1883–85, William Le Baron Jenney), that the complete iron
and steel skeleton was first used. Combined with
improvements in fireproofing, wind bracing and foundation
technology, the skeleton frame made tall buildings possible.

A commercial building in the Chicago School style was
tall in comparison to its predecessors—usually more than 6
stories but fewer than 20. It was rectangular with a flat roof
and terminating cornice. Ornamentation was usually
minimal and subordinated to the functional expression of
the internal skeleton that appeared as a grid of intersecting
piers and horizontal spandrels. Because the exterior walls of a
skeleton-framed structure do not have to bear tremendous
weights, they can have large areas of glass, terra cotta or
other nonsupporting materials. Windows filled a great
proportion of the wall space. Two types of windows were
particularly characteristic of the commercial style. One was
the projecting bay or oriel that ran the full height of the
building, emphasizing the verticality. The other was the so-
called Chicago window composed of a large fixed central
pane flanked by two narrow casements that provided
ventilation. Large display windows usually occupied the
ground-floor level. Above were floors of identical office space.
Facades were organized in a number of ways. Some borrowed
minor elements of Richardsonian Romanesque or Gothic
Revival ornament. The buildings that were more stark and
devoid of ornament now appear the most modern, for they
presaged the mid-20th-century development of glass and
steel skyscrapers.

The architect who developed the best-known and most
distinctive architectural treatment for tall commercial
buildings was Louis Sullivan. His buildings, like a classical
column, had a base consisting of the lower two stories, a
main shaft in which verticality was emphasized by piers
between the windows (occasionally joined by arcading at the
top) and—the crowning glory—an elaborate and boldly
projecting terra-cotta cornice. Besides this basic organization,
Sullivan's buildings can easily be identified by their
distinctive low-relief ornament of intricately interwoven
foliate designs. This remarkably creative ornamentation
usually appeared at the entrance (often an arch), on the
spandrels (horizontal divisions between windows) and on the
cornice.

Along with Jenney and Sullivan, important names in the
development of the tall commercial building include Daniel
H. Burnham, John Wellborn Root, William Holabird, Martin

The Republic Building (1903–05, 1909, Holabird and Roche), Chicago, with its banks of Chicago windows and extremely delicate-seeming structure, is the work of a firm that produced some of the most starkly functional buildings of the Chicago School. (Skidmore, Owings and Merrill)

The Ayer Building (1900, Holabird and Roche), Chicago, clearly reflects its steel frame in the grid pattern of the facade; the walls are composed almost entirely of windows. No superfluous ornament mars the clean lines of the horizontal terra-cotta spandrels. (Cervin Robinson)

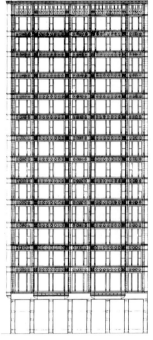

The Reliance Building (1890, 1894, Burnham and Root), Chicago, took advantage of the steel skeletal frame to display large areas of glass, with extraordinary detailing on the terra-cotta spandrels. The projecting oriel windows give the building a soaring quality. (Cervin Robinson)

Roche and Dankmar Adler, Sullivan's partner. A number of people associated with prominent Chicago architectural firms had had engineering experience, which probably helped account for the surge of creative structural advances emanating from the city between 1875 and 1900. Although the structural techniques of the Chicago School spread throughout the country, its stripped, no-nonsense exterior design—in many cases, an extremely personal architectural expression—succumbed to the triumphant academicism of the Beaux-Arts–trained eastern architects who were largely responsible for the 1893 World's Columbian Exposition in Chicago. However, significant buildings of the Chicago School decorative style did appear in many parts of the United States until World War I; the Colcord Building (1910, Robinson and Sheridan) in Oklahoma City is a notable example. ∎

The Prudential (Guaranty) Building (1894–95, Adler and Sullivan), Buffalo, illustrates the early formula for high-rise construction, which divided a building into three parts: a base, a shaft housing identical floors of offices and an elaborate cornice crowning the composition. The elaborate detailing is typically Sullivanesque. (Jack E. Boucher)

BUNGALOWS

The word "bungalow" can be traced to India, where it was used by the British in the 19th century to designate a house type that was one story high and had large, encircling porches. In California the term was applied to houses that, while having the same characteristics of a single story with a porch or porches, owed far more to other antecedents than to anything specifically Indian. Among the immediate ancestors of what came to be known as the California bungalow were the typical small-scale, one-story, Queen Anne–style cottages that had been built in such profusion throughout the state in the 1880s and 1890s. To this basic form architects brought elements of the Craftsman movement, the Stick Style and—in some instances—even a Japanese flavor to produce a distinctly American synthesis.

In the best examples, bungalows display a fine degree of craftsmanship and are constructed of materials left as close as possible to their natural state. Cobblestones, with their rounded shapes prominently displayed, were laid up in foundations and chimneys; walls, whether frame or shingle, were stained a natural shade of brown; and roofs, with their wide overhangs displaying exposed rafters or knee braces, were often of shingle. When the walls were stuccoed, the roof would more than likely be of tile.

In 1909, in his *Craftsman Homes*, Gustav Stickley sought to tell what the style was all about, declaring that a bungalow was "a house reduced to its simplest form," one that "never fails to harmonize with its surroundings, because its low broad proportions and absolute lack of ornamentation give it a character so natural and unaffected that it seems to sing into and blend with any landscape." Stickley further lauded the type by stating that it could "be built of any local material and with the aid of such help as local workmen can afford, so it is never expensive unless elaborated out of all kinship with its real character of a primitive dwelling. It is beautiful, because it is planned and built to meet simple needs in the simplest and most direct way. . . ."

Sears, Roebuck agreed with Stickley and did its part to spread the bungalow gospel by offering several models in its

mail-order catalogs. Sears agreed with the concept of having local workers construct the bungalows, but it differed from Stickley in the matter of materials. Precut lumber, nails, doors and other components were shipped to the site. Thanks to Sears and other building-supply companies, the style spread across the country and regional variations became few and far between.

As befitted the exterior appearance, the bungalow interior, both in plan and detail, was also forthright, direct and functional. Front doors opened directly into living rooms, which were often, in turn, directly connected to the dining room or dining area. In many instances the two spaces were separated only by a half wall. A major element of the interior was the living-room fireplace, emphasized by cobblestones or clinker brick. Ceilings were often beamed, at least in the major rooms, and all wooden surfaces were finished in a natural stain. But if the hearth was the center of the home in winter, in summer the bungalow stretched to the out-of-doors. Glass doors led to porches or terraces that were often covered with pergolas supporting vines.

The bungalow style reached its apogee early in its history, in the work of the brothers Charles S. and Henry M. Greene of Pasadena. Their style transcended the basic bungalow form, however, and it cannot be said that they followed Stickley's dictum of meeting simple needs in the simplest way. The Craftsman tradition, always a part of the bungalow ethic, found its highest expression in their work. The "woodenness" of construction was not only expressed but also emphasized with elegant joinery; beams were not only exposed but also rounded or cut at the angle that would best express both function and beauty. In their work, the bungalow became the western equivalent of the contemporary Prairie Style then being adopted in the middle sections of the country. ■

The Martin Avenue bungalows, Hanchett Residence Park (1910s), San Jose, Calif., are all individual in design, yet they display salient characteristics of the style and relate to each other in overall massing, scale and texture. (Barbara Friedman and John Murphy)

The Irwin House (1906, Greene and
Greene), Pasadena, Calif., is one of
the architects' masterpieces. In some
respects a bungalow on a large scale, it
rests on a stone terrace composed of
natural boulders. Splayed eaves and
strong horizontal lines established by
the balconies give the house a
decidedly Japanese flavor. (Ralston H.
Nagata)

The Longview Farm office (1914, Henry Ford Hoit), Lee's Summit, Mo., shows
many affinities with the bungalow style, including a pergola that eases the
transition between the house and the out-of-doors. (David J. Kaminsky)

The Melville Klauber House (1908–09, Irving J. Gill), San Diego, has Craftsman-style interior features like those adopted in many bungalows, notably the predominance of natural woods. (Marvin Rand)

This Benicia, Calif., cottage is typical of the many built in California in the late 1880s and 1890s. Its irregular plan and elaborate decorative elements seem Queen Anne, but its small size and the prominence of the porch and the shallow pitched gables are forerunners of the bungalow. (Sirlin Studios)

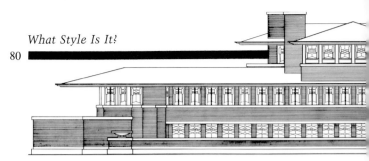

PRAIRIE STYLE

At the start of the 20th century, another group of Chicago architects was at the forefront in the development of a distinctive midwestern residential mode known as the Prairie Style. The acknowledged leader and spokesman of the movement and the architect who produced the most noteworthy examples was Frank Lloyd Wright. A number of young architects, some of whom worked in Wright's studio, also designed in the Prairie Style during its brief but prolific heyday before 1920. They included Walter Burley Griffin, Marion Mahoney, George W. Maher, William E. Drummond, William G. Purcell and George G. Elmslie, to name a few.

The architects of the Prairie School consciously rejected currently popular academic revival styles and sought to create buildings that reflected the rolling midwestern prairie terrain on which they were to be built. As a result, the Prairie house had a predominantly horizontal appearance with a broad hipped or gabled roof and widely overhanging eaves. Often the roof was penetrated by a large, plain, rectangular chimney. Prairie houses generally had two stories with walls of light-colored brick or stucco and wood. Walls were always arranged at right angles—there were no curves in the Prairie house. Dark wooden strips against a light stucco background revealed the influence of traditional Japanese architecture. Windows were usually casements arranged in horizontal ribbons and often featured stained glass in distinctive stylized floral or geometric patterns. One-story porches or porte cocheres, walls and terraces often extended from the main structure of the Prairie house and further emphasized its horizontal appearance.

Interiors were as innovative as the exteriors. The flowing interior spaces of the Queen Anne and Shingle Style were an integral part of Prairie School design. Walls were plain except when accented by wooden strips, as on the exterior. Wooden trim in simple geometric shapes was used for stairways, built-in cabinets and the furniture that some of the architects designed to complement their houses.

The Prairie School had its greatest influence in the Chicago area, where many Prairie Style houses were built in Oak Park and other suburbs. Examples can also be found throughout Illinois, Iowa and Wisconsin, as far east as Rochester, N.Y., and even on the West Coast; they generally were the work of Chicago-based architects. But the ideas of the Prairie School were spread through publications, and Prairie Style houses were designed by architects in Utah and Arizona and as far away as Puerto Rico.

After World War I, Americans embraced the comfortable associations of the revival styles so completely that the Prairie Style did not realize its full potential in the United States. The plans and philosophy of the Prairie School, however, received critical acclaim in Europe through publication of the works of Frank Lloyd Wright. When America was again ready for cautious architectural experimentation in the 1930s, its own Prairie School

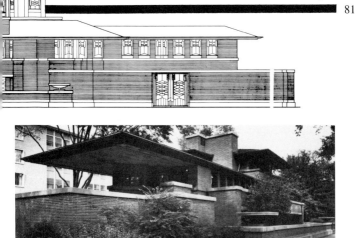

The Robie House (1908–09, Frank Lloyd Wright), Chicago, is perhaps the most famous example of the fully developed Prairie School house. The bold interplay of horizontal planes with the solid vertical mass of the central chimney, along with the cantilevered overhangs, are identifying features of the style. (Janis J. Erins; Cervin Robinson)

The Woodbury County Courthouse (1916–18, Purcell and Elmslie and William Steele), Sioux City, Iowa, is one of the largest Prairie Style buildings ever constructed. Its ornamentation shows some affinity to the work of Louis Sullivan. (Jack E. Boucher)

The Edward Boynton House (1907–08, Frank Lloyd Wright), Rochester, N.Y., was the easternmost example of the Prairie Style when it was built. The chairs and tables in the dining room show that the interiors of Wright's Prairie houses were beautifully integrated with the exteriors. (Hans Padelt)

Merchants' National Bank (Poweshiek
County National Bank) (1914, Louis
Sullivan), Grinnell, Iowa, almost defies
classification. One of a number of
similar small-scale midwestern banks,
its plain brick facade with its
commanding cornice seems related to
the Prairie Style, but the rose window
in its exuberant terra-cotta surround is
unique. (Robert Thall)

movement was dead and the innovative ideas of the style
had to be imported from Europe.

Although the Prairie School had the largest following and
the most influence in the early 20th century, other
important innovations in domestic architecture were made
on the West Coast. There, such pioneering architects as
Bernard Maybeck, Greene and Greene and Irving Gill
developed distinctive styles that survived in a limited way
through the 1930s. They represent a major achievement, one
of international importance, in American architectural
development. However, during the first decades of the 20th
century most Americans chose to live, work and shop in
buildings patterned after architectural styles of the past. ■

PERIOD HOUSES

Georgian Revival, Spanish colonial revival and even revivals of styles that had never been seen in America were popular during the first third of the 20th century, especially for residential architecture. While these houses showed allegiance to one or another design heritage, together their plans, site orientation and general scale were of a piece. Consequently, they can be described by the general stylistic term "period house." This designation indicates that, although differing in style, all period houses identified with the decorative vocabulary of an earlier period.

Styles were suggested by appropriate massing, proportions, materials and a few well-chosen details. The success of the period house depended on its stylistic accuracy. Earlier architects could, in their Queen Anne and contemporary designs, pick bits and pieces from various earlier periods. Now, architects had to become architectural historians in order to successfully suggest a specific earlier period. Most architectural offices had a library with the *White Pine Series* or books on English parish churches or farmhouses in Normandy. The former, a magazine that began as an advertisement series for white pine lumber and developed into a useful reference work, assisted in promulgating the revival of early American architecture by the Historic American Buildings Survey, which began its recording activities in 1933. The first HABS drawings were produced by architects, and the fact that so many of their sheets resemble actual working drawings reflected not only their training, but also their intention that the drawings be used in constructing new houses based on earlier precedents.

The majority of models for period houses were farm or rural structures: English cottages, Spanish haciendas or New England farmhouses. Frequently built on large, newly plotted suburban lots and incorporating many contemporary ideas of interior arrangement and planning, typical period houses were far more spacious than earlier revival structures. Like Shingle Style and Prairie School houses, period houses had an intimate relationship with the landscape. Often sprawling across the width of a lot, period houses had two yard areas, a formal front and an informal back yard. Rarely did a period house not have a rear terrace, porch or patio.

The period house was not an isolated phenomenon. Many churches built at the same time boasted details and

Greystone (1925–28, Gordon B. Kaufman), Beverly Hills, Calif., incorporates details from ages past, but its overall arrangement, expansiveness and close relationship to the landscaping mark it as a period house. (Jack E. Boucher)

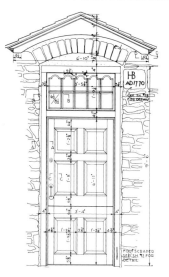

The Hasbrouck House (mid-18th century), Newburgh, N.Y., was recorded in an early HABS project. With drawings such as this, the HABS recorders in the 1930s fostered the popularity of period design. Their careful measurements made possible the authentic reproduction of features such as this doorway. (Daniel M. C. Hopping)

proportions taken directly from examples built centuries before, either in America or in Europe. Another manifestation of the same spirit that produced period houses and churches was the country house. Larger than their city cousins, these mammoth houses were the centers of complexes that included stables, barns, guest houses, gardeners' cottages and similar structures. In the most developed examples, an overall architectural theme pervaded the group. The era that made these estates possible ended in the 1930s, and few of them survive in their original capacity.

The interiors of both period and country houses had fewer rooms than their 19th-century predecessors, but the rooms were much larger and space flowed more freely. Often, especially in smaller period houses, the dining room was replaced by a dining area at one end of an oversized living room—an arrangement reflecting both the open planning and the more informal lifestyle of the times.

Although derived from historical precedent, the period house was a distinctive architectural development that was basically American. And, although the full flowering of the style occurred several decades ago, mutants of the species can be found today along the curving streets of almost any suburban development. ∎

The Warden's House (1926), Federal Reformatory for Women, Alderson, W. Va., is based on English precedent (seen in its half-timbering), but the plan and shape identify the structure as a period house. (Richard Cheek)

Caumsett Manor (1920s, John Russell Pope), Long Island, N.Y., is an exemplary country estate. Its shingle-covered barn complex and Georgian Revival garage are among the carefully designed components of the complex. (Jack E. Boucher)

St. Matthew's Episcopal Church (1910, Willis J. Polk), San Mateo, Calif., a convincing period design in the Gothic mode, displays a number of details based on English medieval prototypes. (Jack E. Boucher)

ART DECO

By the late 1920s, new stylistic influences emanating from Europe had an impact on American architecture, which in general had been little affected by the foliated wanderings of the innovative Art Nouveau of the 1890s and early 20th century. Therefore, Art Deco—or Moderne or Modernistic, as it is variously called—was the first widely popular style in the United States to break with the revivalist tradition represented by the Beaux-Arts and period houses.

Art Deco takes its name from the Exposition Internationale des Arts Décoratifs and Industriels Modernes, held in Paris in 1925 as a showcase for works of "new inspiration and real originality." It was a style that consciously strove for modernity and an artistic expression to complement the machine age. Promotional literature for the "Expo Deco" stated that "reproductions, imitations and counterfeits of ancient styles will be strictly prohibited." This emphasis on the future rather than the past was one of the style's principal characteristics.

Art Deco was essentially a style of decoration and was applied to jewelry, clothing, furniture and handicrafts as well as buildings. Industrial designers created Art Deco motifs to adorn their streamlined cars, trains and kitchen appliances. Art Deco ornamentation consists largely of low-relief geometrical designs, often in the form of parallel straight lines, zigzags, chevrons and stylized floral motifs. In Europe these forms were inspired by Cubism, in America by North and South American Indian art. This ornament could be rich, varied and handcrafted or reduced to the merest suggestion for efficient machine production.

Concrete, smooth-faced stone and metal were characteristic exterior architectural coverings, with accents in terra cotta, glass and colored mirrors. Polychromy, often with vivid colors, was frequently an integral part of the design. Forms were simplified and streamlined, and a futuristic effect was often sought. Although buildings clothed with Art Deco motifs exist throughout the country, the style was particularly popular in New York City. Rockefeller

A Michigan Avenue house, Miami Beach, Fla., displays such Art Deco elements as glass brick, horizontal bands of decoration and projecting lintel courses that afforded some respite from the bright Florida sun. (Walter Smalling, Jr.)

Center (1940, Reinhard and Hofmeister; Corbett, Harrison and MacMurray; Hood, Godley and Foulihoux) is the most spectacular example, but the city is replete with other large office and apartment buildings with applied Art Deco ornamentation.

At its best, the Art Deco style produced a harmonious collaboration of effort by architects, painters, sculptors and designers. This harmony is well illustrated in some of the great movie palaces of the 1920s and 1930s, where curtains, murals and light fixtures bore the same Art Deco motifs as the building itself. Art Deco was a conscious rejection of historical styles and was a popular form of ornamentation. It was, however, scorned by the more intellectual practitioners of a new and even more radically iconoclastic style that began to appear in the 1930s—the International Style. ■

The Pan Pacific Auditorium (1935, Wurdeman and Becket), Los Angeles, has typically curved Art Deco features, such as the entrance facade marked by four pylons carefully scaled to give the building an impressiveness beyond its actual size. (Marvin Rand)

Miami Beach is a treasure trove of Art Deco design. These early 20th-century hotels in the 700 block of Ocean Drive all display various aspects of the style, especially the contrast of smooth-faced walls with details of metal, terra cotta and colored concrete. (Walter Smalling, Jr.)

The Paramount Theater (1931, Timothy Pfluger), Oakland, Calif., is richly decorated with theatrical motifs such as these dancing ladies that grace the north wall of the Grand Lobby. Their stylized robes and faces harmonize with the Art Deco details surrounding them. (Jack E. Boucher)

The W. P. Story Building (1934, Morgan, Walls and Clements), Los Angeles, features bronze gates at the garage entrance that are pure examples of zigzag Moderne, with stylized floral motifs and faces. (Marvin Rand)

The Selig Commercial Building (1931, Arthur E. Harvey), Los Angeles, is luxuriously ornamented with black and gold terra cotta in chevron, spiral and frond designs. (Marvin Rand)

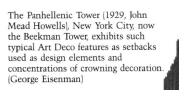

The Panhellenic Tower (1929, John Mead Howells), New York City, now the Beekman Tower, exhibits such typical Art Deco features as setbacks used as design elements and concentrations of crowning decoration. (George Eisenman)

Thomas Jefferson High School (1936, Morgan, Walls and Clements), Los Angeles, has pronounced horizontal banding, curved concave and convex surfaces and vertically articulated piers. (Marvin Rand)

INTERNATIONAL STYLE

In February and March 1932, the Museum of Modern Art in New York City displayed its first architectural exhibition, entitled simply "Modern Architecture." As its catalog stated, the exhibition was intended to prove that the stylistic "confusion of the past 40 years . . . [would] shortly come to an end." Photographs and drawings of works by architects then practicing in similar styles in 15 countries were grouped under the term "International Style." In a book published by the organizers of the exhibition the same year, this new term was used as the title—*The International Style: Architecture Since 1922.*

The International Style is based on modern structural principles and materials. Concrete, glass and steel were the most commonly used materials. While Chicago School architects merely revealed skeleton-frame construction in their designs, International School architects reveled in it. Their rejection of nonessential decoration was perhaps the major difference that distinguished the International Style from the Art Deco. Ribbon windows were a hallmark of the style, as were corner windows, in which the glass was mitered without any corner support. Bands of glass became as important a design feature as the bands of "curtain" that separated them. These strips of windows and solid planes helped create a horizontal feeling, another important aspect of the style, even in high-rise buildings. Here again the International Style differed from Art Deco, which frequently used setbacks, piers and other devices to create a sense of verticality. International Style designers viewed a skyscraper essentially as floors of office space stacked on top of one another.

Artificial symmetry was studiously avoided in the International Style. Balance and regularity, however, were admired and fostered. A tripartite expression of base, shaft and capital—the norm in high-rise construction of the Chicago School—was never used in the International Style. Mundane building components such as elevator shafts and compressors for air conditioning became highly visible aspects of design. The cantilever and ground-floor piers were often used in International Style structures.

Many of the most famous architects who worked in 20th-century America, among them Walter Gropius, Ludwig Mies van der Rohe, Richard Neutra and Marcel Breuer, started their practices in the International Style. American-born architects who practiced in the style include Raymond Hood and George Howe. The latter, in partnership with Swiss-born William Lescaze, designed one of the major American examples of the style—the Philadelphia Saving Fund Society building (1932), known as the PSFS. Many of these architects went on to design in more personal idioms, abandoning the vigorous functionalism of the International Style. However, as a set of principles emphasizing functionalism, stark simplicity and flexible planning, the International Style continues to exert a great influence on modern architecture.

On the assumption that it is impossible to evaluate recent history, this examination of stylistic developments in American architectural history concludes with the 1930s. For now, as Walter Gropius said, we must leave it "to the future historian to settle the history of today's growth in architecture, and get to work and let it grow." ∎

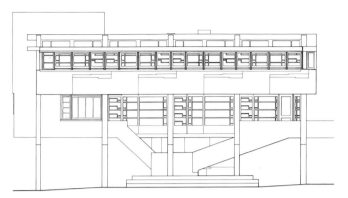

The Lovell Beach House (1926, R. M. Schindler), Newport Beach, Calif., displays remarkable force in its advancing and receding planes and its contrasts of solids and voids yet retains a careful sense of balance. The first floor is essentially an outdoor living space, protected from the elements by the second floor. (Ralston H. Nagata and Stanley A. Westfall; Marvin Rand)

The Hoover House (1919, Arthur B.
Birge Clark), Stanford University,
Stanford, Calif., has sculptural forms,
arched openings and an intimate
relation to the landscape that reflects
California mission design, but its
cubistic forms and strong horizontal
emphasis link it to the International
Style. (Jack E. Boucher)

The Farnsworth House (1949–51), Ludwig Mies van der Rohe), Plano, Ill., is a small-scale International Style design in the architect's later, more personal idiom. (Jack E. Boucher)

Fallingwater (1936, Frank Lloyd Wright), Bear Run, Pa., evokes the tenets of the International Style in its horizontal planes and dramatic cantilevers of reinforced concrete. The overall design and siting, however, mark it as an individual work of genius and one of Wright's most admired designs. (John A. Burns, AIA)

Glossary

This glossary is a guide to common architectural terms. For more precise definitions, consult architectural dictionaries listed in the bibliography.

ADOBE   A sun-dried, unburned brick of earth (generally clay) and straw; a structure made with such bricks.

AISLE   A part of a church parallel to the nave and divided from it by piers or columns; a passageway between rows of seats, such as in a church or auditorium.

ARCADE   A series of arches supported by columns or piers; a building or part of a building with a series of arches; a roofed passageway, especially one with shops on either side.

ARCHITRAVE   The lower part of a classical entablature, resting directly on the capital of a column; the molding around a window or door.

ASHLAR   Hewn or squared stone, also masonry of such stone; a thin, dressed rectangle of stone for facing walls, also called ashlar veneer.

ASTYLAR   Without columns or pilasters.

AXIALITY   Symmetrical disposition of parts of a building or of structures along an axis.

BALUSTER   An upright, often vase-shaped, support for a rail.

BALUSTRADE   A series of balusters with a rail.

BAND WINDOWS   A horizontal series of uniform windows that appear to have little or no separation between them.

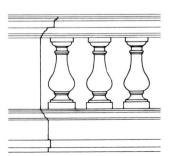

Balustrade

BAPTISTERY A part of a church; formerly, a separate building used for baptism.

BARGEBOARD A board, often ornately curved, attached to the projecting edges of a gabled roof; sometimes referred to as verge-board.

BATTER The receding upward slope of a wall or structure.

BATTLEMENT A parapet built with indentations for defense or decoration.

BAY One unit of a building that consists of a series of similar units, commonly defined by the number of window and door openings per floor or by the space between columns or piers.

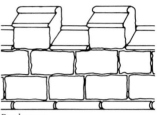

Battlement

BELT COURSE A narrow horizontal band projecting from the exterior walls of a building, usually defining the interior floor levels.

BLIND ARCH An arch that does not contain an opening for a window or door but is set against or indented within a wall.

BRACE A diagonal stabilizing member of a building frame.

BRACKET A support element under eaves, shelves or other overhangs; often more decorative than functional.

BUTTRESS A projecting structure of masonry or wood for supporting or giving stability to a wall or building.

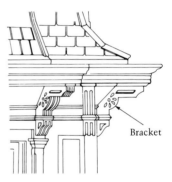

Bracket

CANTILEVER A projecting beam or part of a structure supported only at one end.

CAPITAL The top, decorated part of a column or pilaster crowning the shaft and supporting the entablature.

CARTOUCHE An ornamental panel in the form of a scroll, circle or oval, often bearing an inscription.

CASEMENT A window with sash hung vertically and opening inward or outward.

CASTELLATED Having battlements and turrets, like a medieval castle.

CAST IRON Iron, shaped in a mold, that is brittle, hard and cannot be welded; in 19th-century American commercial architecture, cast-iron units were used frequently to form entire facades.

CHEVRON A V-shaped decoration generally used as a continuous molding.

CHIMNEY POT A pipe placed on top of a chimney, usually of earthenware, that functions as a continuation of the flue and improves the draft.

CLAPBOARD A long, narrow board with one edge thicker than the other, overlapped to cover the outer walls of frame structures; also known as weatherboard.

CLASSICAL Pertaining to the architecture of ancient Greece and Rome.

CLERESTORY The upper part of the nave, transepts and choir of a church containing windows; also, any similar windowed wall or construction used for light and ventilation.

CORBEL A bracket or block projecting from the face of a wall that generally supports a cornice, beam or arch.

Chevron

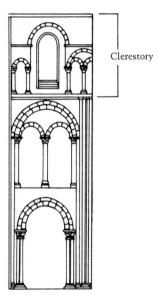

Clerestory

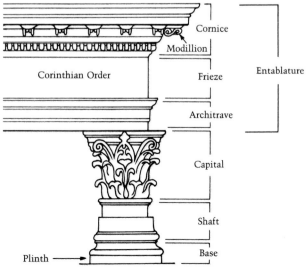

Corinthian Order

Cornice

Modillion

Entablature

Frieze

Architrave

Capital

Shaft

Plinth

Base

CORINTHIAN ORDER The most ornate of the classical Greek orders of architecture, characterized by a slender fluted column with a bell-shaped capital decorated with stylized acanthus leaves; variations of this order were extensively used by the Romans.

CORNICE In classical architecture, the upper, projecting section of an entablature; projecting ornamental molding along the top of a building or wall.

COURSED MASONRY A wall with continuous horizontal layers of stone or brick.

CRENELLATION A battlement.

CROCKET In Gothic architecture, carved projections in the shape of stylized leaves that decorate the edges of spires, gables and pinnacles.

CUPOLA A dome-shaped roof on a circular base, often set on the ridge of a roof.

Crocket

DEPENDENCY A structure subordinate to or serving as an adjunct to a main building.

DORIC ORDER The oldest and simplest of the classical Greek orders, characterized by heavy fluted columns with no base, plain saucer-shaped capitals and a bold simple cornice.

DORMER A vertically set window on a sloping roof; the roofed structure housing such a window.

DOUBLE-HUNG SASH WINDOW A window with two sash, one above the other, arranged to slide vertically past each other.

DOUBLE PORTICO A projecting two-story porch with columns and a pediment.

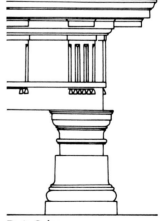

Doric Order

EAVES   The projecting overhang at the lower edge of a roof.

EGG-AND-DART MOLDING   A decorative molding comprising alternating egg-shaped and dart-shaped motifs.

ENTABLATURE   In classical architecture, the part of a structure between the column capital and the roof or pediment, comprising the architrave, frieze and cornice.

EYEBROW DORMER   A low dormer in which the arched roofline forms a reverse curve at each end, giving it the general outline of an eyebrow.

FANLIGHT   A semicircular or fan-shaped window with radiating members or tracery set over a door or window.

FENESTRATION   The arrangement of windows in a wall.

FESTOON   A carved, molded or painted garland of fruit, flowers or leaves suspended between two points in a curve.

FINIAL   An ornament at the top of a spire, gable or pinnacle.

FLEMISH GABLE   A gable with stepped and occasionally multicurved sides, derived from 16th-century Netherland prototypes.

FLUTED   Having regularly spaced vertical, parallel grooves or "flutes," as on the shaft of a column, pilaster or other surface.

FOLIATED   Decorated with leaf ornamentation or a design comprising arcs or lobes.

GABLE A triangular wall segment at the end of a double-pitched or gabled roof.

GALLERY A roofed promenade, colonnade or corridor; an outdoor balcony; in the South, a porch or veranda.

GAMBREL A ridged roof with two slopes on each side, the lower slope having the steeper pitch.

Gambrel

HACIENDA In Spanish-speaking countries or areas influenced by Spain, a large estate, plantation or ranch; also, the house of the ranch owner; in the southwestern United States, a low sprawling house with projecting roof and wide porches.

HALF-TIMBERING Wall construction in which the spaces between members of the timber frame are filled with brick, stone or other material.

HEWN AND PEGGED A frame construction system in which the beams are hewn with an adze (predating saws) and joined by large wooden pegs.

HIPPED ROOF A roof with four uniformly pitched sides.

HOOD MOLDING A large molding over a window, originally designed to direct water away from the wall; also called a drip molding.

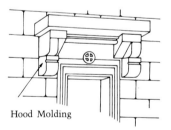

Hood Molding

HORSESHOE ARCH An arch shaped like a horseshoe; common in Islamic architecture.

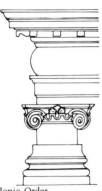

Ionic Order

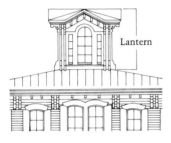

Lantern

IONIC ORDER An order of classical Greek architecture characterized by a capital with two opposed volutes.

LANCET A narrow pointed arch.

LANTERN A structure built on the top of a roof with open or windowed walls.

LEADED GLASS Small panes of glass held in place with lead strips; the glass may be clear or stained.

LEAN-TO A simple structural addition that has a single-pitch roof.

LOZENGE A diamond-shaped decorative motif.

MANSARD ROOF A roof that has two slopes on all four sides.

MASONRY Wall construction of materials such as stone, brick and adobe.

MEASURED DRAWING An exact-scale drawing based on measurements taken from an existing building.

MEDALLION An object resembling a large medal or coin.

MINARET A tall, slender tower attached to a mosque with one or more projecting balconies.

MITER The edge of a piece of material, generally wood, that has been beveled preparatory to making a miter joint.

MODILLION An ornamental bracket or console used in series under the cornice of the Corinthian order and others.

MOLDED BRICK Brick shaped in a mold, commonly in decorative shapes.

MOLDING A continuous decorative band that is either carved into or applied to a surface.

MULLION A vertical member separating (and often supporting) windows, doors or panels set in a series.

NAVE The long, narrow main part of a church that rises higher than the flanking aisles.

NOGGING The brick or rubble material used to fill the spaces between wooden frames.

OBELISK A tall, four-sided shaft that is tapered and crowned with a pyramidal point.

ORDER Any of several specific styles of classical and Renaissance architecture characterized by the type of column used (e.g., Doric, Ionic, Corinthian, Composite, Tuscan).

PALLADIAN WINDOW A tripartite window opening with a large arched central light and flanking rectangular side lights.

PARAPET A low, solid, protective wall or railing along the edge of a roof or balcony.

PATERA A circular ornament used in decorative relief work.

PAVILION A part of a building projecting from the rest; an ornamental structure in a garden or park.

PEDIMENT A wide, low-pitched gable surmounting the facade of a building in a classical style; any similar triangular crowning element used over doors, windows and niches.

PILASTER A shallow pier attached to a wall; often decorated to resemble a classical column.

PLINTH The base of a pedestal, column or statue; a continuous course of stones supporting a wall.

PODIUM A low platform or base.

POLYCHROMY The use of many colors in decoration, especially in architecture and statuary.

PORTAL The principal entry of a structure or wall of a city.

PORTE COCHERE A large covered entrance porch through which vehicles can drive.

PORTICO A major porch, usually with a pedimented roof supported by classical columns.

PRESSED METAL Thin sheets of metal molded into decorative designs and used to cover interior walls and ceilings.

PUEBLO Indian communities in the Southwest with distinctive flat-roofed structures of adobe and stone.

QUOIN Units of stone or brick used to accentuate the corners of a building.

Quoin

REEDED Decoration of parallel convex moldings (the opposite of fluted).

REREDOS An ornamental screen behind an altar.

REVEAL   The vertical side of a door or window opening between the frame and the wall surface.

RINCEAU   A band of ornament consisting of intertwining foliage.

ROCOCO   The decorative style developed from the baroque; characterized by delicacy, light colors and a general reduction in building scale.

ROSETTE   Stylized floral decoration.

RUSTICATION   Masonry cut in massive blocks separated from each other by deep joints.

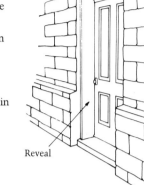

Reveal

S

SALTBOX   A gabled-roof house in which the rear slope is much longer than the front.

SASH   A frame in which the panes of a window are set.

SETBACK   An architectural expedient in which the upper stories of a tall building are stepped back from the lower stories; designed to permit more light to reach street level.

SHAFT   The main part of a column between the base and capital.

SKELETON FRAME   A freestanding frame of iron or steel that supports the weight of a building and on which the floors and outer covering are hung.

SPANDREL   The triangular space between the left or right exterior curve of an arch and the rectangular framework surrounding it; the space between adjacent arches and the horizontal molding or cornice above them; in skeleton frame construction, the horizontal panels below and above windows between the continuous vertical piers.

SPINDLE   A turned wooden element, often used in screens, stair railings and porch trim.

STAIR HALL   A room specifically designed to contain a staircase.

STAIR TOWER   A projecting tower that contains a staircase serving all floors; usually found in castles and chateaux.

STRINGCOURSE A narrow, continuous ornamental band set in the face of a building as a design element; also known as a cordon.

SWAG A festoon in which the object suspended resembles a piece of draped cloth.

TERRA COTTA A fine-grained, brown-red, fired clay used for roof tiles and decoration; literally, cooked earth.

TRACERY The curved mullions of a stone-framed window; ornamental work of pierced patterns in or on a screen, window glass or panel.

TREFOIL A design of three lobes, similar to a cloverleaf.

TUDOR ARCH A low, wide, pointed arch common in the architecture of Tudor England.

TURRET A small, slender tower usually at the corner of a building, often containing a circular stair.

VAULT An arched ceiling of masonry.

VERANDA A roofed open gallery or porch.

VIGA A wooden beam used in a series to support the roof of an Indian pueblo structure; the ends usually project through the outer walls.

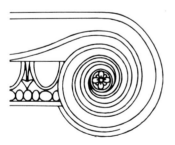

Volute

VOLUTE A spiral, scroll-like ornament.

WATTLE AND DAUB A method of construction with thin branches (wattles) plastered over with clay mud (daub).

WEATHERBOARD Clapboard; wooden siding.

Bibliography

This bibliography lists books dealing with the development of American architecture. Most are of a general nature, but some discuss specific styles. Several architectural dictionaries are included for further explanation of terms in the glossary.

Andrews, Wayne. *Architecture, Ambition and Americans.* New York: Free Press, 1964.

_____. *Architecture in America: A Photographic History from the Colonial Period to the Present.* 1960. Rev. ed. New York: Atheneum, 1977.

Blumenson, John J. G. *Identifying American Architecture: A Pictorial Guide to Styles and Terms, 1600–1945.* Nashville: American Association for State and Local History, 1977. Rev. ed. New York: Norton, 1981.

Brooks, H. Allen. *The Prairie School: Frank Lloyd Wright and His Midwest Contemporaries.* Toronto: University of Toronto Press, 1972.

Burchard, John, and Bush-Brown, Albert. *The Architecture of America: A Social and Cultural History.* Boston: Little, Brown, 1961.

Carrott, Richard G. *The Egyptian Revival: Its Sources, Monuments and Meaning, 1808–1858.* Berkeley: University of California Press, 1978.

Condit, Carl W. *American Building: Materials and Techniques from the First Colonial Settlements to the Present.* Chicago: University of Chicago Press, 1969.

_____. *The Chicago School of Architecture.* Chicago: University of Chicago Press, 1964.

Downing, Andrew Jackson. *The Architecture of Country Houses.* 1850. Reprint. New York: Dover, 1969.

Drexler, Arthur. *The Architecture of the Ecole des Beaux-Arts.* New York: Museum of Modern Art, 1977.

Fitch, James Marston. *American Building: The Historical Forces That Shaped It.* Boston: Houghton Mifflin, 1966.

_____. *American Building 2: The Environmental Forces That Shape It.* Boston: Houghton Mifflin, 1972.

Fleming, John; Honour, Hugh; and Pevsner, Nikolaus. *The Penguin Dictionary of Architecture.* 1966. Rev. ed. Baltimore: Penguin Books, 1983.

Giedion, Sigfried. *Space, Time and Architecture: The Growth of a New Tradition.* 1941. 5th ed. Cambridge: Harvard University Press, 1972.

Girouard, Mark. *Sweetness and Light: The Queen Anne Movement, 1860–1900.* New York: Oxford University Press, 1977.

Gowans, Alan. *Images of American Living: Four Centuries of Architecture and Furniture as Cultural Expression.* 1964. Reprint. New York: Harper and Row, 1976.

Hamlin, Talbot. *Greek Revival Architecture in America.* 1944. Reprint. New York: Dover, 1969.

Hammett, Ralph W. *Architecture in the United States: A Survey of Architectural Styles Since 1776.* New York: Wiley, 1976.

Harris, Cyril M. *Dictionary of Architecture and Construction.* New York: McGraw-Hill, 1975.

Hitchcock, Henry-Russell. *The Architecture of H. H. Richardson and His Times.* 1936. 2nd. ed., rev. Cambridge: MIT Press, 1966.

_____. *Architecture: Nineteenth and Twentieth Centuries.* 1958. 1963. 2nd ed. Reprint. Baltimore: Penguin Books, 1971.

_____. *In the Nature of Materials: The Buildings of Frank Lloyd Wright, 1887–1941.* 1942. Reprint. New York: Da Capo, 1973.

Hitchcock, Henry-Russell, and Johnson, Philip. *The International Style: Architecture Since 1922.* 1932. Reprint. New York: Norton, 1966.

Hunt, William Dudley, Jr. *Encyclopedia of American Architecture.* New York: McGraw-Hill, 1980.

Jordy, William H. *American Buildings and Their Architects. Vol. III: Progressive and Academic Ideals at the Turn of the Twentieth Century.* Garden City, N.Y.: Doubleday, 1972.

_____. *American Buildings and Their Architects. Vol. IV: The Impact of European Modernism in the Mid-twentieth Century.* Garden City, N.Y.: Doubleday, 1972.

Kidney, Walter C. *The Architecture of Choice: Eclecticism in America, 1880–1930.* New York: Braziller, 1974.

Kimball, Fiske. *Thomas Jefferson, Architect.* 1916. Reprint. New York: Da Capo Press, 1968.

Lancaster, Clay. *The American Bungalow, 1880–1920s.* New York: Abbeville, 1984.

Loth, Calder, and Sadler, Julius Trousdale, Jr. *The Only Proper Style.* Boston: New York Graphic Society, 1976.

McCoy, Esther. *Five California Architects.* New York: Reinhold, 1960.

Maass, John. *The Gingerbread Age: A View of Victorian America.* 1957. Reprint. New York: Greenwich House, Crown, 1983.

_____. *The Victorian Home in America.* New York: Hawthorn Books, 1972.

Morrison, Hugh. *Early American Architecture: From the First Colonial Settlements to the National Period.* New York: Oxford University Press, 1952.

Mumford, Lewis. *The Brown Decades: A Study of the Arts in America, 1865–1895.* 1931. Reprint. New York: Dover, 1955.

_____. *Sticks and Stones: A Study of American Architecture and Civilization.* 1924. Reprint. New York: Dover, 1955.

Mumford, Lewis (ed.). *Roots of Contemporary American Architecture: 37 Essays from the Mid-nineteenth Century to the Present.* 1952. Reprint. New York: Dover, 1972.

National Trust for Historic Preservation; Wrenn, Tony P.; and Mulloy, Elizabeth. *America's Forgotten Architecture.* New York: Pantheon Books, 1976.

Naylor, Gillian. *The Arts and Crafts Movement: A Study of Its Sources, Ideals and Influence on Design Theory.* Cambridge: MIT Press, 1971.

Newcomb, Rexford. *Spanish Colonial Architecture in the United States.* Locust Valley, N.Y.: J. J. Augustin, 1938.

Peterson, Charles E. (ed.). *Building Early America.* Philadelphia: Chilton, 1976.

Pierson, William H., Jr. *American Buildings and Their Architects. Vol. I: The Colonial and Neoclassical Styles.* Garden City, N.Y.: Doubleday, 1970.

Placzek, Adolf K. (ed.). *The Macmillan Encyclopedia of Architects.* New York: Macmillan, 1982.

Rifkind, Carole. *A Field Guide to American Architecture.* New York: New American Library, 1980.

Robinson, Cervin, and Bletter, Rosemary Haag. *Skyscraper Style: Art Deco New York.* New York: Oxford University Press, 1975.

Roth, Leland M. *A Concise History of American Architecture.* New York: Harper and Row, 1979.

Saylor, Henry H. *Dictionary of Architecture.* 1952. Reprint. New York: Wiley, 1963.

Scully, Vincent J., Jr. *The Shingle Style and the Stick Style: Architectural Theory and Design from Richardson to the Origins of Wright.* 1955. Rev. ed. New Haven, Conn.: Yale University Press, 1971.

Smith, G. E. Kidder. *Architecture in America: A Pictorial History.* New York: American Heritage, 1976.

Stanton, Phoebe B. *The Gothic Revival and American Church Architecture: An Episode in Taste, 1840–1856.* Baltimore: Johns Hopkins University Press, 1968.

Walker, Lester. *American Shelter: An Illustrated Encyclopedia of the American Home.* New York: Overlook Press, Viking, 1981.

Waterman, Thomas T. *Domestic Colonial Architecture of Tidewater Virginia.* 1932. Reprint. New York: Da Capo, 1968.

Whiffen, Marcus. *American Architecture Since 1780: A Guide to the Styles.* Cambridge: MIT Press, 1969.

Whiffen, Marcus, and Koeper, Frederick. *American Architecture, 1607–1976.* Cambridge: MIT Press, 1981.

Wilson, Richard; Pilgrim, Dianne; and Murray, Richard N. *The American Renaissance: 1876–1917.* New York: Pantheon, 1979.

Winter, Robert. *The California Bungalow.* Los Angeles: Hennessey and Ingalls, 1980.

Information Sources

The following organizations and agencies can provide further information on architects, American architecture and the preservation of historic buildings. For archival and photograph collections on specific architects, consult the resources listed in Further Reading.

American Institute of Architects
1735 New York Avenue, N.W.
Washington, D.C. 20006

American Society of Civil
Engineers
345 East 47th Street
New York, N.Y. 10017

American Society of Landscape
Architects
1733 Connecticut Avenue, N.W.
Washington, D.C. 20009

Cooperative Preservation of
Architectural Records
Prints and Photographs Division
Library of Congress
Washington, D.C. 20540

Historic American
Buildings Survey
National Park Service
U.S. Department of the Interior
Washington, D.C. 20013–7127

Historic American
Engineering Record
National Park Service
U.S. Department of the Interior
Washington, D.C. 20013–7127

National Building Museum
The Pension Building
440 G Street, N.W.
Washington, D.C. 20001

National Register of
Historic Places
National Park Service
U.S. Department of the Interior
Washington, D.C. 20013–7127

National Trust for Historic
Preservation
1785 Massachusetts Avenue, N.W.
Washington, D.C. 20036

Regional Offices

Northeast Regional Office
45 School Street
Boston, Mass. 02110

Mid-Atlantic Regional Office
6401 Germantown Avenue
Philadelphia, Pa. 19144

Southern Regional Office
456 King Street
Charleston, S.C. 29403

Midwest Regional Office
53 West Jackson Boulevard
Suite 1135
Chicago, Ill. 60604

Mountains/Plains Regional
Office
511 16th Street
Suite 700
Denver, Colo. 80202

Texas/New Mexico
Field Office
500 Main Street
Suite 606
Forth Worth, Tex. 76102

Western Regional Office
One Sutter Street
Suite 900
San Francisco, Calif. 94104

Society of Architectural
Historians
1700 Walnut Street
Suite 716
Philadelphia, Pa. 19103

HOW TO USE
THE HABS COLLECTION

The photographs, measured drawings and historical information that form the collection of the Historic American Buildings Survey are housed in the Prints and Photographs Division (Architecture, Design and Engineering Collections) of the Library of Congress in Washington, D.C. The division's reading room is open to visitors and researchers. The records, which may be researched using a printed checklist, card catalog and subject card index, are arranged in geographical order: by state, county, city or vicinity and building or project name. Researchers may consult captioned black and white photographs, written histories and photocopies of measured drawings (not all buildings are recorded in all three forms of documentation). Available illustrations and documentation may be retrieved using file numbers based on geographical location; this number also serves as the negative number used to order prints of HABS photographs. Measured drawings carry numbers assigned by HABS as the documentation is created.

In November 1983 a computerized checklist of buildings in the HABS (and Historic American Engineering Record) collection was published as the first effort to list all buildings and sites in both surveys and as the first national catalog to the HABS collections since a 1941 catalog and 1959 supplement. This checklist is intended to serve as a major guide to the collection, both for researchers using the Library of Congress facilities and for those unable to visit Washington. The checklist, following the geographical arrangement, indicates the amount of documentation available for each building or site and the appropriate file numbers.

Several additional aids are available for researching the collection. The Library of Congress can provide a list of publications about the various state and local surveys conducted by HABS and HAER, including all published catalogs, as well as a list of publications that reproduce substantial portions of the collections. Two publications in microfilm and microfiche also may be ordered, one from the Photoduplication Service of the Library of Congress and one from a private publisher, Somerset House. Researchers may request an information packet from the Prints and Photographs Division providing reading and price lists and basic information on the HABS, HAER and division collections.

Copies of all HABS and HAER materials in the Library of Congress may be ordered from the Photoduplication Service. Those making such requests should provide the names and locations of the buildings and type of documentation desired to the Photoduplication Service, Library of Congress, Washington, D.C. 20540. The library will respond with an order form, building identification numbers, type of documentation available and a price quotation. This order form should be returned with proper payment to the Photoduplication Service. The photographs and measured drawings published in this book, as well as supplemental historical information on the buildings pictured, may be ordered in this manner. (Some recent recording projects may not yet have been transmitted to the library.)

Other Books from The Preservation Press

ALL ABOUT OLD BUILD-INGS: THE WHOLE PRESER-VATION CATALOG. Diane Maddex, Editor. This fact-filled, catalog-style book offers a lively, readable mixture of photo-graphs, drawings, resource list-ings, case histories, excerpts and quotations. It provides a wealth of information organized into 15 major subject areas. 436 pages, illustrated, bibliographies, index. $39.95 hardbound, $24.95 paper-bound.

AMERICA'S COUNTRY SCHOOLS. Andrew Gulliford. The first book to examine the country school as a distinctive building type. Through 400 pho-tographs it captures the histor-ical and architectural legacy of country schools (from dugouts and soddies to frame buildings and octagons) and provides ideas for preserving them. 296 pages, illustrated, appendixes, index. $18.95 paperbound.

ARCHABET: AN ARCHITEC-TURAL ALPHABET. Photo-graphs by Balthazar Korab. Here is a new way of looking at architecture—through the eyes and imagination of an award-winning photographer in search of an alphabet in, on and around buildings. Juxtaposes dramatic photographs with quotations from architectural observers from Goethe to Frank Lloyd Wright. 64 pages, illus-trated. $14.95 hardbound.

BUILT IN THE U.S.A.: AMERI-CAN BUILDINGS FROM AIR-PORTS TO ZOOS. Diane Maddex, Editor. Building Watch-ers Series. A guidebook-sized history of 42 American building types with essays by noted authorities explaining the forms as a response to the functions. 192 pages, illustrated, bibliogra-phy, appendixes. $9.95 paper-bound.

MASTER BUILDERS: A GUIDE TO FAMOUS AMERI-CAN ARCHITECTS. Introduc-tion by Roger K. Lewis. Building Watchers Series. In brief, well-illustrated essays noted authori-ties examine the style and en-during landmarks of 40 major American architects. 204 pages, illustrated, bibliography, appen-dixes, index. $9.95 paperbound.

RESPECTFUL REHABILITA-TION: ANSWERS TO YOUR QUESTIONS ABOUT OLD BUILDINGS. Technical Preser-vation Services, U.S. Depart-ment of the Interior. This book answers 150 questions property owners and residents most fre-quently ask about rehabilitating old houses and other historic buildings. The answers are based on the Secretary of the Interior's Standards for Rehabili-tation, which are reprinted in full. 200 pages, illustrated, bibli-ography, glossary, appendixes. $12.95 paperbound.

To order Preservation Press books, send the total of the book prices (less 10 percent discount for National Trust members), plus $3 postage and handling, to: Preservation Shop, 1600 H Street, N.W., Washing-ton, D.C. 20006. Residents of California, Massachusetts, New York and South Carolina, please add applicable sales tax. Make checks payable to the National Trust or provide credit card number and signature.